I0479152

The Millionaire Blueprint

Unlocking Wealth with
the Law of Attraction

Tony Tushar Popat

Welcome

Welcome to my book! My name is Tony Tushar Popat, and I am thrilled to share my story and insights with you. This book is the culmination of my life's experiences and my journey towards finding success and happiness.

Purpose of the Book:

The purpose of this book is to inspire and motivate readers to achieve their goals and dreams. I believe that everyone has the potential to lead a fulfilling life, but often, we are held back by our limiting beliefs and circumstances. Through this book, I aim to share the principles and techniques that have helped me overcome my challenges and achieve success.

Target Audience:

This book is for anyone who is struggling to find direction in their life or is seeking guidance on how to overcome obstacles and achieve success. Whether you are a student, a professional, an entrepreneur, or someone looking to make a change in your life, this book is for you.

What to Expect:

In this book, I share my personal journey towards success and happiness, and the lessons I have learned along the way.

You will learn about the Law of Attraction and how to use it to manifest your desires, the power of positive thinking, the importance of setting goals, and how to develop a growth mindset.

You will also learn about the challenges I faced growing up in a middle-class family in India, my struggles with finances, and how I overcame them to build a successful business. I will share my insights on entrepreneurship, leadership, and the importance of taking calculated risks.

Conclusion:

I hope that this book will inspire and motivate you to take action towards your goals and dreams. Remember, success is not an overnight achievement, but a journey that requires persistence, hard work, and a positive mindset. So, let's embark on this journey together, and I promise that you will not regret it.

About the author

The author's name is Tushar Popat, also known as Tony: A story of overcoming financial struggles and embracing the Law of Attraction.

Born in 1970 in Mumbai, India, he grew up in a middle-class family. Eventually, they moved to the town of Surat in the state of Gujarat on the west coast of India. Life was tough for him and his family. His father attempted several businesses throughout his life, but most of them failed, barely covering the household expenses. Despite this, his parents believed in the value of good education and sent him and his siblings to the best school in town, even though they could not afford the high fees of an English-medium school. Many others would put their children in local language schools, but his parents wanted them to have the best education possible.

His parents believed that with good education, their children would have a better life and a brighter future. They were right, as all of the kids are doing well now. However, their journey was not without struggles. They had to overcome the shadows of their parent's bad luck, or so they thought, until they discovered the power of the Law of Attraction.

He embraced the Law of Attraction, which is the belief that positive thoughts can lead to positive outcomes. By focusing on positive thoughts and energy, he was able to overcome the financial struggles of his past and achieve success in his life. He attributes much of his success to his mindset and the power of positive thinking.

Despite the challenges that he faced in his early life, he persevered and found success through hard work, determination, and a positive attitude. His story serves as an inspiration to others who may be struggling to overcome obstacles in their own lives. With the right mindset and a belief in the Law of Attraction, anyone can achieve their dreams and live a fulfilling life.

Table Of Contents

Chapter 1. Introduction:

A. Overview of the Law of Attraction

The Law of Attraction is a powerful concept that states that like attracts like. In other words, your thoughts and emotions have a direct impact on what you attract into your life. This includes your experiences, relationships, financial situation, and overall well-being.

According to the law of attraction, the universe is constantly responding to your thoughts and emotions, and it sends back to you experiences and situations that match your dominant vibration or frequency. So, if you are constantly thinking about lack and scarcity, you will attract more of that into your life. But if you focus on abundance and positivity, you will attract more of that into your life as well.

One of the key principles of the law of attraction is that you are the creator of your own reality. Your thoughts and emotions shape your experiences and determine what you attract into your life. By taking control of your thoughts and emotions, you can start to create the reality you want.

The law of attraction has been discussed in various spiritual and philosophical traditions, and has been popularized in recent years through books, movies, and seminars. While the concept may seem simple, it can be challenging to put into practice, especially if you have long-standing limiting beliefs or negative thought patterns.

In this book, we will explore the law of attraction in greater detail, and provide you with practical, actionable steps you can take to start applying it in your own life. Whether you want to attract more wealth, improve your relationships, or achieve your dreams, the law of attraction can help you get there.

B. The Millionaire Mindset

The Millionaire Mindset refers to the beliefs, attitudes, and habits that are common among successful and wealthy individuals. These individuals think and act differently than the average person, and they approach life and business with a unique set of principles and strategies.

One of the key elements of the millionaire mindset is a focus on abundance and positivity. Millionaires believe that there is always enough, and they approach life with a sense of abundance and gratitude. They also have a growth mindset, meaning they believe that they can always learn and grow, and that their success is not limited by their current circumstances or abilities.

Another important aspect of the millionaire mindset is a strong sense of self-awareness and personal responsibility.

Millionaires take ownership of their lives and their outcomes, and they are not afraid to take risks and pursue their passions. They are also resilient, and they know how to overcome setbacks and challenges with determination and persistence.

In addition to these key traits, millionaires also have specific habits and routines that help them maintain their success. These may include things like regular exercise, meditation, goal setting, and continuous learning and growth.

By adopting the millionaire mindset, you can start to think and act like a successful, wealthy individual. This will not only help you attract more abundance and prosperity into your life, but it will also help you lead a more fulfilling and meaningful life. So if you want to become a millionaire, the first step is to adopt the millionaire mindset.

C. Manifesting Your Dreams: Bianca's Journey to Winning a Car

Bianca is a resident of Mumbai who had gone with her husband and son to her vacation home, a bungalow in Lonavala, a picturesque hill station in the outskirts of the city. One day, while her husband was away on an errand, she received an unexpected phone call from a representative of a TV shopping channel. The caller informed her that she had won a car from Tata Motors, one of India's leading automobile manufacturers. Bianca was overjoyed and could not believe her luck. The caller asked her for her bank account details so they could transfer the prize money of INR 1.2 million if she preferred that instead of the car.

Bianca was hesitant to share her bank account details with a stranger, as she had always been cautioned by her husband against such calls. She requested the caller to wait for ten minutes until her husband returned home, and then she would provide them with her account details. The caller agreed and promised to call back in ten minutes.

Bianca could hardly contain her excitement and immediately called her husband to share the incredible news. When he returned home, she told him everything, and they both started planning how they would use the prize money. However, her husband cautioned her that the call was probably a scam and not to get her hopes up too high. She was initially dismissive of his suspicions, as the caller had provided accurate details about her purchase from the shopping channel.

Still, to be on the safe side, Bianca called the TV shopping channel to verify the caller's claims. To her dismay, she learned that the call was indeed a scam. The channel was running a promotion at the time, and the top prize was a scooter, not a car. Moreover, the winner of the scooter would receive it in person, on live television, to prove that the promotion was genuine.

After this experience, Bianca thought that her chances of winning a car were nil but she never gave up in her heart. She had been dreaming of owning a brand new car for a long time. She visualized every detail, from the smell of a new car to the feeling of driving it every day, to work and shopping, and everywhere. She would often spend time imagining herself driving the car, feeling the wind in her hair and the joy in her heart. And the feeling of winning a new car for free was something she could only dream of until now.

She had always wanted to own a Mahindra XUV 500. So, she saved up her money and finally bought one. While negotiating for the accessories, the Sales Rep showed her a contest to apply online which she did after buying the car when she returned home with the help of her son.

Three months later, she received a phone call that would change her life. It was from the sales agent of the car dealership they were negotiating with. He informed her that she had won the first prize in a company-sponsored competition, and the prize was a brand new Mahindra KUV 100!

Bianca was initially skeptical, but the sales agent sent her an email confirming her win, and she was elated to learn that she had indeed won a car. The car was a Mahindra KUV 100, and it was a compact SUV perfect for her and her son while the larger XUV 500 can be used by her husband. Though they still had to pay the taxes, the car was free.

When she finally won a car in a company-sponsored competition, she was overjoyed and grateful. Her dream had finally come true, and she knew that her positive vibes and belief in the universe's ability to manifest her desires had played a significant role in her win. It was a reminder that the power of positive thinking can make anything possible.

Bianca attributed her good fortune to the law of attraction. She believed that her positive vibes and excitement about winning a car had sent a message to the universe, and it had manifested in the form of her winning the car. She shared her story with many people, and some of them followed her example of positive thinking and experienced similar good luck.

In conclusion, Bianca's story teaches us to be cautious when we receive unsolicited phone calls from strangers claiming to offer us prizes or benefits. However, it also shows us the power of positive thinking and believing in the universe's ability to manifest our desires.

Chapter 2. Understanding the Power of Thoughts

The Science of Attraction: Understanding the Science Behind the Law of Attraction

The law of attraction is often considered a spiritual or philosophical concept, but there is actually a scientific basis for how it works. In recent years, the field of quantum physics has provided new insights into how the universe and our minds interact, and this has helped to validate the principles of the law of attraction.

One of the key principles of quantum physics is that everything in the universe is made up of energy. This includes our thoughts, emotions, and even physical objects. According to quantum physics, our thoughts and emotions emit a vibration or frequency that can influence the physical world around us.

The law of attraction works by matching our thoughts and emotions with similar vibrations or frequencies in the universe. This is known as the principle of resonance. When we focus our thoughts and emotions on abundance, positivity, and success, we emit a high-frequency vibration that attracts more of the same into our lives.

In addition to the principle of resonance, quantum physics also supports the concept of entanglement. This principle states that everything in the universe is connected, and that our thoughts and emotions can influence not only our own experiences, but also the experiences of others.

The science behind the law of attraction is still in its early stages, and there is much more to be learned. However, the existing research provides strong evidence that our thoughts and emotions have a real and measurable impact on our lives.

The Power of Thoughts and Emotions

One of the most important aspects of the law of attraction is the role that our thoughts and emotions play in shaping our reality. Our thoughts and emotions create a vibration or frequency that attracts experiences and situations that match that frequency.

For example, if you are constantly thinking about lack and scarcity, you will attract more of that into your life. On the other hand, if you focus your thoughts and emotions on abundance and prosperity, you will attract more of that into your life.

It is important to note that the law of attraction is not a magic bullet, and it will not immediately solve all of your problems. However, by changing your thoughts and emotions, you can start to shift your energy and vibration, and this can help you attract more of what you want into your life.

C. The Role of Visualization

Visualization is one of the most powerful tools for applying the law of attraction in your life. Visualization involves creating a mental image of what you want to experience or achieve, and then focusing on that image as if it were already real.

By visualizing what you want, you activate the power of your mind and emotions, and you start to attract experiences and situations that match your vision. Visualization also helps you to focus your thoughts and emotions on abundance and success, which can help you overcome limiting beliefs and negative thought patterns.

There are many different techniques for visualization, and you may find that one technique works better for you than another. Some common techniques include creating a vision board, using affirmations, and writing your goals.

In addition to visualization, it is also important to take physical actions that align with your goals. The law of attraction is not a passive process, and it requires you to take action in order to see results. However, by combining visualization with physical action, you can create a powerful and synergistic effect that can help you achieve your goals faster and more effectively.

In the next section, we will explore some of the specific tools and techniques you can use to apply the law of attraction in your life, and start attracting more abundance and success.

D. Manifesting My American Dream: The Power of Law of Attraction in Bringing Me to the Land of Opportunities.

We are four siblings - my elder sister, myself, my younger sister, and our youngest sister. Our family had moved out of Mumbai and stayed in a place called Valsad for about a year at my uncle's, my dad's elder brother's home. My dad was looking for a business opportunity using the savings he had from Mumbai. After he bought a business in Surat, we were all set to move there. However, my elder sister was so attached to my aunt, my uncle's wife, that she decided to stay back in Valsad and not move with us to Surat. Despite my parent's initial concerns, they agreed to let her stay with our aunt until we were settled in the new town. They assured her that they would come back for her or arrange for her to be brought to Surat later. Little did they know that she would end up growing up in Valsad at my uncle's house until she was an adult. But more on that later.

We moved to Surat and started our new life there. It was a small rental apartment with just two rooms - one serving as the kitchen and the other as the living room and bedroom combined. Although the space was limited, we were content and happy in our new home. Our community was bustling with children, and after school, we would all gather in the compound to play and have fun.

However, my father had faced several failures in his business ventures, and he was always anxious about the success of his business. Looking back now, I understand that his constant fear and negative mindset were the reasons behind most of his business failures. As I learned later in life, our thoughts, beliefs, and feelings have the power to shape our reality, and my parents' pessimistic outlook attracted more difficulties into their lives. Financial struggles were a constant part of our lives until my father's passing.

After my father's death, my mother found solace in the company of her elder sister, my Aunt Jyoti Masi, who had a completely different mindset. Her positive attitude and outlook towards life slowly began to influence my mother, and she started changing her perspective towards money, success, and happiness. A few years later, when my Aunt Jyoti Masi passed away, she left behind a considerable inheritance for my mother, including two homes in Mumbai, which is one of the most expensive cities in India. She also left behind investments, stocks, jewelry, and other belongings, which brought financial comfort to my mother. It was a turning point for her, and she started to embrace the concepts of the law of attraction that my siblings and I had been sharing with her. When my mother passed away a few years ago, she had left behind a legacy of financial abundance, all because of her newfound understanding of the power of thoughts, beliefs, and feelings.

As for me, I had my own share of struggles when I moved out of my home for work. However, it was through the principles of the law of attraction that I was able to transform my life completely.

One of the most significant instances was when I set my sights on coming to America. I had always been fascinated by the United States as a land of dreams, thanks to the Hollywood movies I had grown up watching. The cities in the US seemed so beautiful, with their tall buildings, fancy cars, clean roads, and flyovers crisscrossing each other. The Hollywood stars were larger than life in my eyes, with their handsome boys, pretty girls, and thrilling action scenes. I was particularly enamored with action movies of hollywood stars and also James Bond movies. Whether they were British or Hollywood productions - they were all the same to me as a kid. As I grew older, the desire to come to America grew stronger in me.

I met a friend in my hometown Surat who had recently moved to the US for higher studies. He shared his experiences, and I was even more intrigued by the opportunities and possibilities that the US offered. I started visualizing myself living in America, working in a high-rise building, and exploring the American way of life. I read books on personal development, mindset, and the law of attraction, and I began to apply these principles in my daily life.

I started setting clear goals, creating vision boards, and taking inspired actions towards my dream of moving to the US. Despite facing numerous challenges and setbacks, I remained focused and persistent in my pursuit of my American dream.

Me and my best friend Brad were the pioneers in Surat, India to become certified as Microsoft Certified Systems Engineers (MCSE). It was a significant achievement and garnered a lot of attention in our community. I was thrilled to have acquired such a prestigious certification and it opened up new opportunities for me.

I then relocated to Mumbai, where I began teaching MCSE at two different institutions as an instructor. I thoroughly enjoyed sharing my knowledge and skills with eager students who were keen to excel in the field of IT. However, I aspired for more and wanted to explore different avenues to further my career.

Luck was on my side as I landed a permanent job at a company called eindia.com during the dot-com boom era. The company was developing and promoting a portal, and I was entrusted with the responsibility of managing their IT infrastructure. I set up servers, configured routers, managed email servers, databases, and web servers, among other tasks. It was a challenging yet rewarding experience, and I was proud of the impact I made in shaping the company's technological landscape.

Meanwhile, my friend Brad had managed to secure a US tourist visa based on his family's textile business in Surat. He established the necessary documentation to prove his status as a businessman, and he was soon on his way to the United States. Unfortunately, I didn't have enough documentation to support my visa application, and my US dream was put on hold.

Not one to be discouraged, I then moved to Bangalore and secured a job as a Network and Systems Administrator for a small dot-com startup called QMAGS.com. The company specialized in creating PDF searchable magazines that could be subscribed to online. I was responsible for setting up their entire IT infrastructure, from configuring leased line routers to managing Microsoft Exchange servers for email, MS SQL servers for databases, and IIS web servers for hosting internal websites. My work was well-received, and the company sent me to their office in Hong Kong for a month to set up servers there as well.

Hong Kong was a whole new world for me. It felt like stepping into a scene from the Hollywood movies I had seen, with its stunning buildings, sleek cars, and well-maintained roads. However, I soon realized that language could be a barrier as most people on the streets didn't speak English. Nevertheless, I embraced the experience and completed my work successfully.

Upon my return to the Bangalore office, I was thrilled when the company offered me the opportunity to visit the US to set up their servers in a data center. It felt like a dream come true, and I eagerly accepted the opportunity. I made all the necessary arrangements, packed my bags, and embarked on my journey to the United States with a sense of excitement and anticipation. It was a significant milestone in my career, and I was determined to make the most of this opportunity to further my professional growth and fulfill my American Dream.

My journey to the United States began with a business visa that lasted for a month. I stayed at a comfortable motel called Comfort Inn, which was conveniently located just a short walk away from the workplace where our company had hired a consultant to work on software, hardware, and network setups. Together, we worked tirelessly to set up servers at a massive datacenter called Exodus, located south of the Bay area. It was my first time witnessing such a large datacenter, and it was an awe-inspiring experience.

After successfully setting up the servers and getting the site up and running, I returned to Bangalore with the hope of getting another opportunity to travel to the US. However, that opportunity never came. Instead, I received a job offer from GE Capital in Hyderabad, which I decided to accept. I moved there and eventually got married. My wife and I then applied for a tourist visa at the US consulate with the plan to visit the US for a vacation. Fortunately, we were granted the visa and were excitedly looking forward to our trip.

A year after our marriage, I received a call from one of my roommates from Bangalore who informed me that he was visiting India and wanted to meet up. He was staying in our old apartment in Bangalore, where some of our old friends still lived. So, I drove with my wife to Bangalore to meet him. During our reunion, my friend told me that he had a business in the US and offered me a job. Intrigued, I considered the opportunity. However, my wife was expecting our child, and we had a tradition that the wife always goes to her mom for delivery, so I dropped her off there and took a flight to the US with my friend Vicky.

Upon arriving in the US, I faced a setback as I was informed that I couldn't get a visa to work officially, but I could work unofficially in their warehouse, picking merchandise and delivering. Unsure of what to do, I discussed my predicament with my friend Vicky. Over the weekend, we attended a dinner party hosted by Vicky's friend, Aaron, at his home. During our conversation, I shared my situation with Aaron, who mentioned that he knew someone who owned an IT company and could potentially offer me a job on an H1B visa. Intrigued, I agreed to meet this person, named Carl (not real name), who indeed offered me a job as a windows admin and filed my H1B visa, which was eventually approved.

I worked for Carl for a few months before receiving another job offer from a company owned by David. I decided to accept the offer and joined the new company. Meanwhile, my wife had given birth to a baby girl and did not want to travel to the US when the baby was too young. So, after a year, my wife and daughter joined me in the US, and we moved into an apartment in Edison, New Jersey. I then received a new job offer from a company owned by Abby, who was known for his kindness. I accepted the offer and even received a slight raise. And that marked the beginning of my new life in the US.

One day, as I was rummaging through one of my old bags, I stumbled upon a forgotten treasure - a pocket diary from years ago. Flipping through its pages, I came across something that caught my attention. It was a wish I had written down long ago - a desire to go to the US and settle down there. In that moment, it hit me - my wish had come true. The universe had granted my request, and I hadn't even realized it.

Reflecting on my life, I realized that all the events and circumstances that had unfolded were leading me towards this very moment. I had been so caught up in the hustle and bustle of everyday life that I had forgotten to appreciate the small things I once cherished in India. The clean roads, the nice cars - I was driving a minivan at the time, which seemed so ordinary to me now, but back in India, it would have been considered a luxury with its automatic doors, power windows, auto headlight shutoff, auto dimmer in the rearview, and leather seats. I was living the dream I had wished for, and I hadn't even realized it.

I looked around and saw so much more to appreciate. It was snowing outside my window, and it was a sight I had never witnessed in India. Even though there are a few places in India where it snows, like Kashmir, I had never had the chance to experience it firsthand. But here I was, marveling at the beauty of the snowfall. I had a loving wife, a cute daughter, a job, and I was happy. I thanked God for all that I had been blessed with in my new home.

It was a humbling moment for me, realizing that my wish had been planted in the universe, and it had been working its magic all along. It made me pause and appreciate the journey that had brought me to where I was. I vowed to cherish every moment, big or small, and never take anything for granted. My life in the US was truly a dream come true, and I was grateful for the opportunities and blessings that had come my way. I learned to look beyond the challenges and hardships and see the beauty in the everyday moments, for they were the ones that made my life truly magical. With a heart full of gratitude, I embraced my life in the US as my own little piece of heaven on earth.

Moving to America was not easy. I faced cultural differences, language barriers, and homesickness. However, I remained committed to my goals and continued to apply the principles of the law of attraction in my daily life. I stayed positive, surrounded myself with like-minded individuals, and worked diligently towards my academic and career goals.

Over time, I found success in my career. I landed a job with a renowned company, and eventually obtained permanent residency in the US.

Looking back, I realized that the power of thoughts, beliefs, and feelings had played a significant role in transforming my life. The law of attraction had helped me manifest my dream of living in America, and it had become a fundamental part of my mindset and lifestyle.

As for my elder sister, she eventually joined us in Surat after completing her education. She too had embraced the principles of the law of attraction and had found success in her career as a successful entrepreneur. She often spoke about how her positive mindset and outlook had helped her overcome challenges and achieve her goals.

Today, our family is spread across different parts of the world, pursuing our dreams and living abundant lives. We credit our success to the understanding and application of the law of attraction, which had transformed our lives from struggling to thriving.

In conclusion, our family's journey has been a testimony to the power of thoughts, beliefs, and feelings in shaping our reality. Despite facing challenges and setbacks, we learned to harness the law of attraction to manifest our dreams and create the life we desired. It has been an incredible journey of personal growth, resilience, and abundance, and we are grateful for the life-changing impact of the law of attraction in our lives.

Chapter 3. How to Train Your Brain to Think Like a Millionaire

A. Identifying and Changing Limiting Beliefs

One of the first steps in training your brain to think like a millionaire is to identify and change any limiting beliefs that may be holding you back. Limiting beliefs are negative thought patterns that prevent you from achieving your goals and reaching your full potential.

Examples of limiting beliefs include beliefs about money being scarce or hard to come by, or beliefs that you are not smart enough or capable enough to succeed. These beliefs can be deeply ingrained, and they can be difficult to change.

However, changing your limiting beliefs is essential if you want to train your brain to think like a millionaire. The law of attraction is based on the principle that you attract what you focus on, so if you focus on scarcity and lack, you will continue to attract those experiences into your life.

To change your limiting beliefs, you need to start by becoming aware of what you are thinking and feeling. Pay attention to your thoughts and emotions throughout the day, and write down any negative or limiting thoughts that come to mind.

Next, examine each limiting belief and ask yourself if it is truly serving you. If not, replace it with a positive, empowering belief that supports your goals and your vision of abundance and success. For example, instead of believing that money is hard to come by, you can believe that there are always opportunities for abundance and that you have the skills and abilities to attract prosperity into your life.

B. Developing a Growth Mindset

In order to train your brain to think like a millionaire, it is also important to develop a growth mindset. A growth mindset is a way of thinking that embraces challenges and sees failures as opportunities for growth and learning.

People with a growth mindset believe that their abilities and intelligence can be developed through hard work and perseverance. They are not afraid of challenges, and they see failure as a stepping stone to success.

On the other hand, people with a fixed mindset believe that their abilities and intelligence are set in stone and cannot be changed. They are often afraid of challenges, and they see failure as a reflection of their inherent lack of talent or intelligence.

To develop a growth mindset, focus on your effort and progress rather than your results. Celebrate your small wins, and see challenges and failures as opportunities to learn and grow. Embrace new experiences and embrace change, and remember that your abilities and intelligence are not fixed, but can be developed and strengthened with time and effort.

C. Cultivating a Positive Mental Attitude

A positive mental attitude is another key component of thinking like a millionaire. Millionaires are typically optimistic and have a positive outlook on life, even in the face of challenges and setbacks.

To cultivate a positive mental attitude, focus on the positive aspects of your life and your experiences. Look for the good in every situation, and practice gratitude by expressing appreciation for what you have. Surround yourself with positive and supportive people, and avoid negative or toxic relationships.

In addition, adopt positive self-talk, and avoid negative self-criticism. Be kind and compassionate to yourself, and focus on your strengths and accomplishments rather than your weaknesses and failures.

Finally, practice mindfulness and meditation to help you maintain a positive mental attitude, and reduce stress and anxiety. Mindfulness and meditation can help you focus your thoughts and emotions, and increase your overall well-being and happiness.

D. Setting and Achieving Goals

Setting and achieving goals is a fundamental aspect of thinking like a millionaire. The ability to set clear and achievable goals is what sets successful people apart from the rest. Millionaires are highly goal-oriented, and they understand the importance of having a clear vision of what they want to achieve. They don't just dream about their goals; they take concrete steps to make them a reality.

To begin with, setting goals is the first step towards success. It gives you a sense of direction and purpose, and it helps you prioritize your time and energy towards achieving your objectives. However, merely setting goals is not enough. You need to have a plan of action to achieve them. Millionaires understand this and create a roadmap that outlines the steps they need to take to reach their desired destination.

Another crucial element of setting and achieving goals is breaking them down into smaller, more manageable milestones. This helps in keeping track of progress and staying motivated along the way. Setting short-term goals and achieving them can provide a sense of accomplishment and keep you on track towards reaching your long-term goals.

Moreover, successful people understand that achieving goals requires discipline and perseverance. It takes hard work, focus, and a commitment to doing whatever it takes to achieve success. They don't let setbacks or obstacles deter them from their goals, but instead, use them as learning opportunities to grow and improve. They are willing to put in the extra effort and go the extra mile to achieve their desired outcomes.

Finally, achieving goals requires a willingness to take risks and step outside of your comfort zone. Millionaires understand that success is not achieved by playing it safe, but by taking calculated risks and making bold moves. They are not afraid of failure, and they use it as a learning opportunity to improve and come back stronger.

In conclusion, setting and achieving goals is a fundamental aspect of thinking like a millionaire. Successful people understand the importance of having a clear vision and creating a roadmap to achieve their objectives. They break down their goals into smaller milestones and use setbacks as learning opportunities. They have a willingness to take risks and step outside of their comfort zone, and they are committed to doing whatever it takes to achieve their desired outcomes. By adopting these principles, anyone can think like a millionaire and achieve their goals in life.

E. The Power of Visualization: How I Landed My Dream Job at Wells Fargo - Alok Bajpai

Today marks one month since I joined Wells Fargo as a project manager, and it wouldn't have been possible without the power of visualization. It's a reminder to never underestimate what you can achieve with a clear vision and commitment. When I first applied for the position, I spent time visualizing myself in the role, envisioning myself succeeding and making a positive impact on the team. This practice not only gave me the motivation to pursue the job but also allowed me to approach the position with a clear understanding of what I wanted to achieve. With a strong vision in mind, I was able to commit fully to the job, putting in the necessary effort and energy to ensure success. Looking back on my first month, I can confidently say that my visualization practice played a crucial role in my success thus far. As I continue on this journey, I hope that my story can inspire others to never underestimate the power of visualization and the impact it can have on achieving your goals.

I'm an avid supporter of self-help literature, journals and books. It's a great way to conduct personal development activities and become the best version of yourself.

My life was forever changed when I stumbled upon Think and Grow Rich by Napoleon Hill at a recycler's. It's amazing that something which was intended for disposal could spark such a meaningful journey for me.

In India, when you have newspapers and magazines that you no longer need but don't want to throw away, it's a great idea to recycle them. You can make some money by selling these items to someone who comes door-to-door in your area. It's a great way to benefit the environment while gaining something in return.

Amidst the pile of books, magazines and waste papers otherwise known as "Ruddy" in India, I discovered the life-changing book "Think and Grow Rich", a source of lasting inspiration. Even though the book was lacking a few pages, my friend's father graciously allowed me to take it from Ruddy. It was his kind gesture that made me realize how even something small and seemingly insignificant can have a positive impact on one's life.

Reading has been a game-changer in my life since I started. Initially, I wasn't at all influenced by self-help books or even general books. But once I began picking them up and reading, my life drastically changed for the better. In addition to being interested in Indian scriptures and reading my books, I'm also taking the time to delve into many self-help books that could help me in personal growth.

When I arrived in the USA in 1999, I started expanding my literary horizons and reading a variety of books. I admire and look up to Oprah, Dr Deepak Chopra, and the late Dr Wayne Dyer for all the wonderful contributions they have made to society. Their books have helped countless people on their journey of self-discovery and enlightenment, and I am deeply grateful for all their hard work. Oprah, Deepak Chopra and the late Dr. Wayne Dyer have all contributed greatly to the world of personal growth and spirituality. Their words have inspired millions of people, providing guidance and insight into the human experience. They have written extensively on topics ranging from happiness to success, helping readers find meaning in their lives and giving them the tools to achieve their goals. We can all be grateful for their timeless wisdom, which will remain with us long after these great teachers are gone.

Reading books is one of life's great joys. It can provide a source of knowledge and entertainment, as well as a way to explore new ideas and perspectives. However, after finishing a book, it can be difficult to remember the insights that were gained from it. That's why I realized the importance of saving books with me forever - so that I can revisit them anytime and gain further insight from them.

For me, reading books is more than just entertainment – it's a way to learn and grow. I try to take the lessons I learned in those books and put them into practice in my life. After reading a book, I'm usually in a trance-like state as I think about how to apply what I've learned. By doing this, I have been able to foster personal growth and development that wouldn't have been possible without these books.

My curiosity about the world around me has grown exponentially over the past few years, and I have become increasingly fascinated with discovering new ideas and exploring different perspectives. I take a deep dive into topics that particularly interest me, using research and creativity to gain a deeper understanding of these areas. With each discovery, my fascination for life only grows stronger.

Tushar Popat's journey to the United States in 2003 was one filled with excitement and uncertainty. Little did he know that his first day would be filled with adventure and surprise when he accidentally lost his passport at the airport. Despite this hiccup, Tushar's determination to pursue his dreams in the US never ceased. Years later, he is now the author of a successful book, and I am proud to call him my friend.

Tushar worked with me we worked together he was one of my best salesperson and the good thing is we created a bond during those three years and we would share our knowledge of I would teach him whatever I knew and you know he would impart his knowledge on me

Working with Tushar was an incredible experience. During our three years together, we developed a strong bond built on mutual respect and admiration. He was one of my best salespeople and always eager to learn, allowing me the opportunity to share my knowledge with him. The connection we made during that time was invaluable – it allowed us both to grow professionally and personally. We forged a strong bond over the three years we worked together, exchanging knowledge and advice as we went. Our partnership was invaluable in helping us both reach our goals and grow professionally.

Over the past two decades, our friendship has been tested and proven. From the days when my friend left my company in 2006 to now, his transformation from a small-time employee to a successful entrepreneur is an inspiring success story. He has certainly outdone himself in his journey and I am proud of what he has achieved in life. With a successful career spanning two industries, he has shown a versatility and ambition that is unmatched. He has become a highly regarded real estate agent and an expert in the field of information technology, allowing him to combine his passion for property with his expertise in IT. A true professional, he has accomplished incredible feats in both domains throughout his career.

I am writing this short story to illustrate the power of visualization, which I learned from him. Visualization is a powerful tool that can help us manifest our deepest desires. It may sound like a fantasy, but the truth is that it's one of the most effective methods for achieving success. By visualizing what we want to achieve, and focusing our energy on those things, we can create the life we desire. With this simple yet powerful tool, anyone can unlock their potential and turn dreams into reality.

He is a person who approaches his work with a great deal of passion and dedication, consistently putting forth his best effort to achieve outstanding results.

I vividly remember my friend Tushar reading "The Secret," and what made him stand out was not just that he read it, but he fully absorbed and integrated its teachings into his life and shared it with his entire family. Witnessing this, he taught me the immense value and power of visualization, and I have utilized this technique many times and achieved countless successes. Recently, I embarked on a new challenge of pursuing a career in project management and decided to take the PMP exam, which is known to be quite challenging if one is not from that domain. As I was preparing for this exam, Tushar and I regularly spoke, and he continually emphasized the significance of visualization. I initially failed the exam due to my overconfidence, but I quickly realized my mistake and decided to put serious effort into my preparation. Eventually, on December 1, 2022, I passed the PMP exam, thanks to the power of visualization and Tushar's unwavering support and encouragement.

Tushar's teachings and his emphasis on visualization have had a profound impact on my life. I have used visualization many times and have achieved many things. One of the most recent successes is my new job at Wells Fargo Bank. I had always visualized myself working for Wells Fargo, and now that dream has become a reality.

Every morning when I drove to the gym, I would see the Wells Fargo sign and visualize myself working there. It was a strange feeling, but I kept telling myself that I would work there one day. Even though I'm not superstitious, I still believe that there's some kind of power in visualization.

I became a customer of Wells Fargo in 2000, just a year after I came to the United States. I've been a loyal customer ever since. When I was looking for a job, I asked my daughter who works for Bank of America to help me, but things didn't work out. So, I decided to keep visualizing and telling myself that I would work for Wells Fargo.

Although I had been confirmed to start working at Wells Fargo on December 22, 2022, the start date kept getting delayed. I was feeling disappointed and hopeless, but I kept visualizing and telling myself that I would work there eventually. After waiting for more than two months, I finally started my new job as a business technology lead/project manager on February 13, 2023.

During the two months and 13 days that I waited, I kept giving interviews and did well in most of them. However, I always had a feeling that my dream job was at Wells Fargo. Even when I was offered other positions, I turned them down because I knew that Wells Fargo was where I was meant to be.

The power of visualization is real, and I have seen its effects in my own life. If you have a dream or a goal, close your eyes and visualize yourself achieving it. See yourself doing what you want to do, and feel it as if it has already happened. Keep visualizing every day, and eventually, you will achieve your goal.

As Napoleon Hill said, "What the mind can conceive and believe, it can achieve." So, don't give up on your dreams, no matter how far-fetched they may seem. With the power of visualization, anything is possible.

In conclusion, I want to thank Tushar for teaching me the value of visualization. Without his guidance and inspiration, I would not have achieved my dream job at Wells Fargo. I hope that my story will inspire others to believe in themselves and the power of visualization. Whatever your goal may be, keep visualizing, keep believing, and you will achieve it. - Alok Bajpai.

Chapter 4. The Importance of Visualizing Your Goals

A. What is Visualization?

Visualization is the process of creating mental images of your goals and desires in your mind. When you visualize, you imagine yourself experiencing your goals as if they have already happened. This helps to activate the power of the law of attraction and bring your goals closer to reality.

Visualization is a powerful tool that can help you to overcome obstacles, increase your motivation, and achieve your goals more quickly and easily. By visualizing your goals, you can create a strong and positive connection to them, which can help you to stay focused and motivated, even when challenges arise.

B. The Science Behind Visualization

The science behind visualization is rooted in the concept of neuroplasticity, which is the idea that the brain can change and adapt in response to experiences and stimuli. When you visualize your goals, you are creating new neural pathways in your brain, and these pathways can help to change your thoughts, beliefs, and behaviors in a positive way.

Research has shown that visualization can activate similar areas of the brain as physical experiences, which can help to create a stronger connection to your goals and increase your motivation to achieve them. This can lead to improved performance, increased confidence, and greater success in achieving your goals.

C. The Benefits of Visualization

Visualization can provide a wide range of benefits, including:

Increased motivation: When you visualize your goals, you can increase your motivation and drive to achieve them. This is because visualization helps to create a stronger connection to your goals, and makes them feel more real and attainable.

Improved focus: Visualization can also help you to maintain focus and stay on track with your goals. By regularly visualizing your goals, you can keep them at the forefront of your mind and avoid becoming distracted or discouraged by obstacles.

Reduced stress and anxiety: Visualization can also help to reduce stress and anxiety by providing a sense of calm and relaxation. When you visualize your goals, you can feel more confident and in control, which can help to reduce stress and anxiety.

Improved performance: Visualization can also lead to improved performance by helping you to see yourself as a successful and confident individual. By visualizing yourself in your desired state, you can improve your mental and emotional state, which can lead to better performance and greater success.

D. How to Visualize Your Goals

To get the most out of visualization, it is important to practice regularly and make it a part of your daily routine. Here are some tips for visualizing your goals effectively:

Find a quiet and relaxing place to visualize:

Find a quiet and relaxed place where you can be alone with your thoughts. Close your eyes, take a few deep breaths, and let yourself relax.

Create a clear and vivid image:

Create a clear and vivid image of your goals in your mind. Imagine yourself experiencing your goals as if they have already happened. Use all of your senses to make the image as real and vivid as possible.

Focus on your emotions:

Focus on the emotions that you want to feel when you achieve your goals. Imagine how it will feel to be successful, confident, and happy. Allow yourself to fully immerse in these emotions and let them guide your visualization.

Repeat regularly:

Repeat your visualization regularly, especially in the morning and before you go to sleep. The more you practice, the stronger your connection to your goals will become.

Visualization can be a powerful tool for achieving your goals and manifesting abundance and success. By incorporating visualization into your daily routine, you can train your brain to achieve your goals.

Visualizing Success: How Sarah Achieved Her Dreams:

Once upon a time, there was a woman named Sarah who had always dreamed of becoming a successful entrepreneur. She had tried starting several businesses in the past, but they all failed. Sarah was feeling discouraged and didn't know what to do next.

One day, while browsing through a bookstore, she came across a book on visualization. The book explained how to use the power of visualization to achieve your goals. It suggested that you should see your goal as a movie in your mind and create a scene where you have already achieved your goal. You should feel the emotions of success and truly believe that you have achieved it.

Sarah was skeptical at first but decided to give it a try. She began by visualizing herself as the CEO of her own successful company. She would picture herself walking into a beautiful office building with her name on the door. She would see herself giving presentations to investors and hiring employees.

As Sarah continued to visualize her success, something amazing happened. She started to believe that her dream was possible. She felt a renewed sense of energy and motivation, and she began to take action towards her goal.

Sarah started attending networking events and talking to potential investors. She would picture herself in her movie scene and feel the confidence and excitement of achieving her goal. Soon enough, Sarah's hard work paid off. She secured funding for her business and was able to open her own office.

As Sarah continued to visualize her success, she found that things just seemed to fall into place. She attracted the right employees, landed important contracts, and her business started to grow rapidly.

Looking back, Sarah realized that visualization was the key to her success. It helped her to believe in herself and gave her the motivation to keep going even when things got tough. By visualizing her success, Sarah was able to achieve her goals and create the life she had always dreamed of.

In conclusion, visualization is a powerful tool that can help you achieve your goals. By creating a mental movie scene of your goal achieved and feeling the emotions of success, you can truly believe that your dream is possible. As Sarah's story shows, visualization can give you the motivation and confidence to take action towards your goals and ultimately lead to success.

Chapter 5. Creating a Vision Board

A. What is a Vision Board?

A vision board is a physical representation of your goals, dreams, and aspirations. It is a collage of images, quotes, and affirmations that represent what you want to achieve and who you want to become. A vision board is a tool for manifestation, helping you to bring your goals closer to reality by focusing your mind on what you want to achieve.

B. How to Create a Vision Board

Gather materials: Gather materials such as magazines, scissors, glue, and a large poster board. You can also use digital tools to create a virtual vision board.

Identify your goals: Start by identifying your goals, dreams, and aspirations. What do you want to achieve in different areas of your life, such as career, relationships, health, and personal growth?

Collect images and quotes: Browse magazines and websites to find images and quotes that represent your goals and aspirations. Cut out images and quotes that resonate with you and capture the essence of what you want to achieve.

Create your vision board: Arrange the images and quotes on your poster board in a way that feels meaningful to you.

Make sure to place your vision board in a location where you will see it regularly, such as your bedroom or workspace.

Refine and update your vision board: Review your vision board regularly and make changes as necessary. Add new images and quotes as you discover them, and remove any items that no longer align with your goals.

C. The Benefits of a Vision Board

Increased motivation: A vision board can increase your motivation and drive to achieve your goals by keeping them at the forefront of your mind.

Improved focus: A vision board can also help you to stay focused on your goals and avoid becoming distracted or discouraged by obstacles.

Enhanced creativity: Creating a vision board can also be a creative outlet, allowing you to tap into your imagination and express your goals in a unique and personal way.

Increased manifestation: A vision board can also help to bring your goals closer to reality by focusing your mind on what you want to achieve. When you see your vision board regularly, you are sending a powerful message to your subconscious mind, which can help to manifest your goals more quickly and easily.

D. Conclusion

Creating a vision board is a simple and effective way to manifest your goals and bring them closer to reality. By focusing your mind on what you want to achieve, you can increase your motivation, improve your focus, and enhance your manifestation abilities. Make creating a vision board a part of your manifestation practice and watch your dreams become a reality.

E. Bringing Abundance to Life with a Vision Board

David was a man with big dreams. He wanted to live in a beautiful house with a big garden, drive a luxurious car, and travel the world. However, he felt that he was stuck in his job, living paycheck to paycheck, and struggling to make ends meet. That's when he discovered the power of visualization and the magic of the vision board.

David started by creating a vision board, just like the book recommended. He cut out pictures of his dream house, the car he wanted to drive, and destinations he wanted to visit. He even included a picture of himself in front of his dream house with a big smile on his face.

Every morning and every evening, David would look at his vision board and imagine himself living in that beautiful house, driving that luxurious car, and traveling to those destinations.

He felt the excitement and joy of achieving his goals as if they had already come true.

Slowly but surely, things started to change for David. He got a promotion at work and started earning more money. He saved every penny he could and made wise investments that allowed him to accumulate wealth faster than he ever thought possible.

Finally, after years of hard work and dedication, David achieved his dream. He found the exact same house that was on his vision board. He bought it and moved in with his family, feeling grateful and proud of his accomplishment. He also bought the same luxurious car that he had envisioned and traveled to the destinations on his vision board.

David realized that creating a vision board had not only helped him achieve his goals, but it had also changed his mindset. He was no longer stuck in a limiting belief system that he couldn't have the life he desired. He was now empowered to manifest his dreams and live the life he always wanted.

In conclusion, creating a vision board is a powerful tool for manifestation. It allows you to focus your mind on your goals and dreams, and it can help you achieve them faster than you ever thought possible. By following the steps outlined in the book, anyone can create a vision board and watch their dreams become a reality.

F. The Law of Attraction in Action: How My Vision Board Helped Me Win $500,000

John had always been fascinated with the idea of winning the lottery. He would often daydream about what he would do with the money and the freedom it would bring. However, he knew that his chances of winning were slim to none. That is until he discovered the power of visualization and the vision board.

John had been practicing the art of visualization for months. He had created a vision board filled with images of the things he desired most in life. He would look at his vision board every morning and night, focusing his mind on his goals and visualizing himself achieving them. He felt the feelings of joy and gratitude as if he had already won the lottery.

One day, as John was driving home from work, he stopped at a gas station to buy a soda. While he was waiting in line, he decided to buy a lottery ticket. He closed his eyes and visualized the winning numbers appearing on the ticket. He felt the excitement and joy of winning as if it had already happened.

Days passed, and John almost forgot about the lottery ticket he had purchased. But one morning, he woke up to a phone call that would change his life forever. He had won the lottery, and the prize was $500,000.

John was in shock, but he knew that his visualization and the vision board had played a huge role in his win. He had been focusing his mind on winning the lottery for months, and his mind had become aligned with his desire. The universe had responded by bringing him the money he had been visualizing.

With the money, John was able to pay off his debts, buy a new car, and travel the world. He was grateful for the power of visualization and the vision board, which had helped him achieve his biggest dream. From that day on, he continued to practice visualization and used the vision board to manifest other desires in his life.

G. Visualizing Prosperity: The Power of a Vision Board. Story of Richard in his own words.

"For as long as I can remember, I have always had a desire to become financially successful. However, despite my best efforts, it always seemed like I was just scraping by. It wasn't until I discovered the power of a vision board that I truly began to see my dreams come to fruition.

I started my vision board journey by collecting images of my financial goals. I found pictures of luxurious homes, fancy cars, and exotic vacations. I even added quotes and affirmations to keep me motivated. I arranged all of these pictures on a poster board, creating a collage that represented my ideal financial future.

Every day, I spent a few minutes focusing on my vision board. I would close my eyes and imagine myself living in the luxurious home, driving the fancy car, and taking those exotic vacations. I visualized these things as if they were already a part of my life, with belief and feelings.

As time passed, I noticed changes in my life. I became more motivated and focused on achieving my financial goals. I started taking action towards building a better financial future. I was more disciplined with my spending habits and I began to see my bank account grow.

One day, I received a job offer that was beyond my wildest dreams. It was a job that paid well and offered opportunities for growth and advancement. With the help of my vision board, I manifested this job into my life. I was amazed at the power of visualization and manifestation.

My vision board not only helped me achieve my financial goals but also improved my overall well-being. It increased my motivation, focus, and positivity. I was more in control of my life and had the power to create the future I desired.

In conclusion, creating a vision board is a simple and effective way to manifest your financial goals. By focusing your mind on what you want to achieve, you can increase your motivation, improve your focus, and enhance your manifestation abilities. Incorporating a vision board into your manifestation practice can help you bring your dreams to life."

Chapter 6. Visualizing in a Half-Trance State

A. What is a Half-Trance State?

A half-trance state is a state of relaxation and focus that is achieved by slowing down your breathing (Hear Rate Variability) and relaxing your body. This state is characterized by reduced external stimuli, allowing you to focus more effectively on your internal thoughts and visualizations. When you visualize in a half-trance state, you are able to bring your subconscious mind into alignment with your conscious goals, increasing your ability to manifest your desires.

B. How to Visualize in a Half-Trance State

Find a quiet, comfortable place: Find a quiet, comfortable place where you can relax and be undisturbed.

Relax your body: Begin by slowing down your breathing and relaxing your body. You can do this by tensing and releasing different muscle groups, starting with your feet and working your way up to your head.

Focus on your visualization: Close your eyes and focus on your visualization. Imagine yourself in a scenario where your goal has already been achieved. See yourself in vivid detail, experiencing the emotions and sensations of having achieved your goal.

The VSS mode, short for Very Still State mode, refers to a stage of meditation where one aims to achieve complete physical stillness, much like a motionless rock. This state is crucial as it allows you to enter the alpha wave state, during which your mind emits alpha waves that facilitate manifestation. The deeper you go into the alpha state, the greater your ability to connect with the universe and manifest your desires. Therefore, achieving the VSS mode can be immensely beneficial for those seeking to harness the power of meditation for self-improvement and personal growth.

Hold the visualization: Hold the visualization for several minutes, allowing your mind to fully immerse itself in the scenario. As you hold the visualization, imagine the goal becoming more and more real, until it feels as though it is happening in the present moment.

Bring yourself back to the present moment: Gradually bring yourself back to the present moment, feeling grateful for the experience and the positive feelings that it has brought to your life.

During the visualization process when you are ending it you need to see that someone in the visualization, not you but some third party person your friend or someone is congratulating you on your achievement and you say thank you.

As the director of your life, it is crucial to approach your visualization process as if you are directing a movie. Imagine creating a scene that captures the moment of achieving your goal or receiving an award. Visualize every detail, from the people around you to the sound of applause as you walk up on stage to receive your award. Create a mental video clip of the scene, starting from the beginning and ending with gratitude. See yourself confidently walking up the stage, receiving the award, turning around to face the audience, and thanking them. Repeat this visualization process as many times as needed until the scene feels real, clear, and vivid. This technique can be applied to any goal, whether it's a one-minute scene or a 30-second clip. With practice, your visualization skills will improve, and you'll be able to manifest your dreams and goals with ease. Remember to always end your visualization with gratitude and appreciation, as this will help you attract more abundance and positivity into your life.

To effectively visualize and manifest your goals, it's important to get into the alpha wave state of your mind. This state can be achieved through regular practice, and is most commonly achieved during the half-trance mode when you're about to sleep. However, it is also possible to enter this state anytime during the day. To get into the alpha wave state, you need to close your eyes and sit very still in a comfortable position. Try to focus in between your eyebrows with your eyes looking a little bit upwards, and just keep focusing there.

Within a few seconds, you will find yourself in your alpha state. As you focus, you will gradually enter the alpha wave state, which makes you more receptive to receiving messages from the universe. In this state, you can demand what you want and the universe will align circumstances and events to facilitate your goals. By regularly entering the alpha wave state and visualizing your goals with clarity, you'll be able to manifest your desired reality with ease.

C. The Benefits of Visualizing in a Half-Trance State

Increased manifestation: If you're looking to amplify your manifestation efforts, consider visualizing your goals in a half-trance state. Doing so can help align your subconscious mind with your conscious desires, resulting in a state of heart-brain coherence. This alignment between your feelings and aspirations can work wonders in bringing your goals closer to reality. By harnessing the power of visualization and heart-brain coherence, you can pave the way for greater success and fulfillment in life.

Improved focus: By slowing down your breathing and relaxing your body, you can improve your focus and concentrate more effectively on your visualization.

Enhanced visualization skills: Regular visualization in a half-trance state can help to improve your visualization skills, making it easier for you to focus on your goals and bring them closer to reality.

Increased confidence: By regularly visualizing yourself in scenarios where your goals have already been achieved, you can increase your confidence and self-belief, making it easier to take action towards your goals.

D. Conclusion on half-trance state.

Visualizing in a half-trance state is a powerful manifestation tool that can help you to bring your goals closer to reality. By slowing down your breathing and relaxing your body, you can focus more effectively on your visualization, bringing your subconscious mind into alignment with your conscious desires. Make visualization in a half-trance state a regular part of your manifestation practice and watch as your goals become a reality.

E. The Hook Method:

The hook method is a powerful technique that can help you harness the power of the Law of Attraction to achieve your goals and create the life of your dreams. The technique involves three simple steps that you can practice every day to attract abundance and prosperity into your life.

Step 1 is to think about the best moment in your life that has happened and you cherish that moment. It could be a moment of immense joy, accomplishment, or love. It could be a moment that made you feel like you were on top of the world. This moment represents your highest emotional state, and you want to use it to anchor your visualization.

In your visualization session, start by recalling this moment and reliving it in your mind. Remember how you felt, what you saw, what you heard, and what you were thinking at that moment. Try to immerse yourself fully in the experience and feel the same emotions again.

Once you are in this state of positive emotion, the next step is to immediately think and visualize the thing you desire or want in life, that is your goal. It could be anything – a new house, a dream job, a loving relationship, financial abundance, or anything else that you desire. Visualize the goal as vividly and clearly as you can with the utmost detail. See yourself already having achieved it. Imagine how you will feel, what you will see, what you will hear, and what you will be thinking when you have achieved your goal. The more you repeat your visualizations every day, the more vivid and clear will your visualization become of your goal and you will start feeling as if it is so real that it is happening with you right now.

After you have visualized your goal, the third step is to feel happy about this goal in your visualization and show gratitude to the universe. You have to be thankful that you have already achieved your goal in your visualization as it will look so real. Express your gratitude by saying "thank you" and feeling the emotions of gratitude and joy. Feel as if you have already received your desire and express your appreciation for it. This will help to align your vibration with the frequency of abundance and attract more of what you desire into your life.

All the three steps need to be repeated once daily when you are going to bed and you close your eyes, it needs to be in the half trance state where you are feeling sleepy and are about to sleep but you try to visualize and at the end of the visualization you go to sleep. The thought will remain in your mind and in your dreams throughout the night and will be connected to the universe. The universe will start to mobilize all the situations, circumstances and things in perfect order for you to be able to achieve your goal. They will all look like coincidences to others, but you know that every step is taking you closer to your goal. It is because of your thoughts, beliefs, and feelings that you are getting closer to your end goal.

When you get up in the morning, you need to feel happy and thankful to the universe for giving you what you had asked for in the goal. The feeling of gratitude and joy will keep you in a positive state of mind and help you attract more of what you desire into your life.

By following the hook method, you can tap into the power of the Law of Attraction and attract abundance and prosperity into your life. With practice and persistence, you can develop a wealth and money mindset that will help you achieve your goals and live the life of your dreams.

F. If you want to predict your future, define it.

Knowing where you are and what brought you here is essential. Now, let's take a step forward and talk about your Point B. Where do you want to end up? What does your ideal life look like? To predict your future, you must define it. I had a mentor who once said, "If you want to predict your future, define it," and those words have stuck with me ever since. This is your chance to define your future, in detail. What kind of house do you want to live in, and how many bedrooms does it have? What color is it, and what does it smell like in the morning? Can you hear the sound of the ocean or birds chirping outside your mountain home? What does your car look like in the driveway? How much time will you spend on your business, and how much time will you spend at home? Will you take the kids to school, hit the gym, or meditate with yoga?

The more details you write down, the more clearly you'll understand what you want, and the universe will be better equipped to help you get there. You must be as specific and detailed as possible to achieve your desired outcome. This exercise is about painting a vivid picture of your ideal life, and it will help you create a blueprint for your life's journey. Visualize your dream life as if it were a movie, with you as the main character, living the life you always wanted. You must believe in this vision wholeheartedly, as though it were already real.

You may have doubts and fears, but when you allow yourself to visualize the life you desire, you will begin to believe it is possible. You will start taking the necessary steps towards making it a reality. The key is to stay focused on your vision and trust in the process. Keep your thoughts positive and allow yourself to receive all the good that is coming your way. The power of positive affirmations is real, and it will help you achieve your goals faster than you ever thought possible.

Now is the time to put your vision into words. Write down every detail of your perfect day, from the moment you wake up to the moment you go to bed. Be specific and detailed, as this will help you create a roadmap towards your desired outcome. This exercise will also help you stay motivated and focused, even when things get tough. Remember, every success story begins with a vision, and it's up to you to create yours. Define your future, and watch as the universe conspires to make it a reality.

Chapter 7. Ask and Ye shall receive.

The law of attraction is a powerful force that can bring our desires to fruition, but it requires us to take action and ask for what we want. It is said that the universe is constantly listening to our thoughts and feelings, and when we put out positive energy and ask for what we want, the universe responds in kind.

Asking for what we want may seem like a simple concept, but many of us struggle with it. We may fear rejection or feel like we don't deserve what we want. However, it's important to remember that we are worthy of our desires, and asking for what we want is a crucial step in manifesting our dreams.

One of the most effective ways to ask for what we want is through visualization. Visualization involves imagining our desired outcome in detail and feeling as if it has already happened. When we visualize our desires, we create a strong emotional connection to them, and this energy attracts more of what we want into our lives.

Another powerful way to ask for what we want is through affirmations. Affirmations are positive statements that we repeat to ourselves to reinforce our beliefs and desires. By stating our desires as if they have already happened, we shift our mindset to one of abundance and attract more of what we want into our lives.

It's also important to take action towards our goals. The universe responds to our energy and effort, so we must be willing to put in the work to achieve our desires. This means taking small steps each day towards our goals, even if they seem insignificant at first. These small actions build momentum and attract more opportunities for us to manifest our desires.

However, it's important to remember that asking for what we want doesn't guarantee that we will receive it. Sometimes, the universe has a different plan for us, or we may not be ready for our desires yet. When this happens, it's important to trust in the process and have faith that everything is working out for our highest good.

In conclusion, asking for what we want is a crucial step in manifesting our dreams. It requires us to shift our mindset to one of abundance, take action towards our goals, and trust in the process. By utilizing visualization, affirmations, and taking small steps each day, we can attract more of what we want into our lives and create a life we love. Remember, the universe is constantly listening, so ask and ye shall receive.

Believe to Achieve: How Mike Turned His Dream into Reality through the Power of Asking

Mike had been working in a corporate job for years, feeling stuck and unfulfilled. He had always dreamed of starting his own business and being his own boss, but he didn't know where to start. One day, he stumbled upon an article about software as a service (SaaS) and how it could help businesses automate and grow. That's when an idea struck him - what if he created a SaaS product that would help small businesses automate their processes and make more money?

Mike knew he had a long road ahead of him, but he was determined to make it happen. He spent countless hours researching and learning everything he could about SaaS and how to create a successful product. He also started networking and attending events to meet like-minded individuals who could help him bring his vision to life.

One day, Mike came across an opportunity to partner with a talented software developer. With his help, Mike was able to create a website that offered a SaaS product that was easy to use and affordable for small businesses. He poured his heart and soul into the project, working tirelessly to ensure its success.

There were many challenges along the way, but Mike kept his focus on the end goal. He believed that his product would be a game-changer for small businesses and that it would generate more than his job, allowing him to quit and pursue his dream of being an entrepreneur full-time.

After months of hard work and dedication, Mike's website finally launched. He started marketing it aggressively, and soon, he began seeing a steady stream of users signing up. Over time, his user base grew, and his website became the go-to platform for small businesses looking to automate their processes and increase their revenue.

Thanks to his perseverance and belief in his vision, Mike's website was making more than his job within a year. He knew it was time to take the leap and quit his job to focus on his business full-time. It was a scary decision, but he had faith in himself and his product.

Today, Mike is a successful entrepreneur, running his own company and helping small businesses all over the world. He's grateful for the opportunity to turn his dream into a reality and for the power of asking and believing.

In conclusion, Mike's story teaches us the importance of asking for what we want and believing that it's possible. When we have a clear vision and work hard towards our goals, the universe has a way of aligning itself to help us achieve them. It's important to stay focused on the end goal, even when faced with challenges and setbacks, and to have faith in ourselves and our abilities.

Chapter 8: Plot Armor - The Unbreakable Shield of Your Life Story

In every story, there is always a hero who faces challenges, adversaries, and obstacles along their journey. These challenges could be in the form of powerful enemies, dangerous monsters, fierce wars, or dire circumstances that seem insurmountable. Yet, despite all odds, the hero emerges victorious, unscathed, and triumphant. Have you ever wondered how this is possible? How is it that the hero always manages to escape unharmed or find a way to overcome seemingly impossible situations?

The answer lies in the concept of "plot armor." Just like in a novel or a story, where the protagonist is protected by an invisible shield that keeps them safe from harm, you too have a plot armor in your own life story. It is a powerful force that safeguards you against any harm or danger that may come your way.

Let's take the example of the famous fictional character, Harry Potter. As a young child, he faced many life-threatening situations at the hands of Lord Voldemort, one of the most powerful dark wizards of all time. However, despite his vulnerability and lack of experience, Harry Potter always managed to escape unharmed. This can be attributed to the plot armor that J.K. Rowling, the author of the Harry Potter series, crafted for her character. It was an invisible shield that protected Harry Potter from any harm, ensuring that he survived and ultimately emerged victorious.

In the same manner, you are the director and author of your own life story. You have the power to create your own plot armor, a shield that will protect you from any challenges or obstacles that may come your way. With this unbreakable shield, you can navigate through life's challenges with confidence, knowing that you are invincible and nothing can harm you.

But how do you believe that you have a plot armor in your life? How do you make it invincible? It all starts with your mindset and perspective. You need to shift your belief system and adopt a positive mindset that views challenges as opportunities for growth and improvement. Instead of seeing obstacles as threats, see them as stepping stones towards your success. Embrace the belief that every problem you face is actually arming you with more power and making you a better version of yourself.

For example, let's say you encounter a setback at work, such as a project not going as planned or facing criticism from your colleagues. Instead of feeling defeated, remind yourself that this setback is just a temporary challenge that will ultimately make you stronger and wiser. Embrace the opportunity to learn from the experience, hone your skills, and come back even more resilient.

Similarly, in your personal life, if you face a difficult situation such as a breakup, a loss, or a health issue, remind yourself that you have a plot armor that will protect you. Trust that you have the inner strength and resilience to overcome any adversity and come out even stronger on the other side.

It's important to note that having a plot armor doesn't mean that you will never face challenges or difficulties. Life is full of ups and downs, and everyone faces obstacles at some point. However, what sets you apart is how you perceive and respond to these challenges. When you believe that you have a plot armor, you shift your perspective from victimhood to empowerment. You stop seeing challenges as roadblocks and start seeing them as opportunities for growth and self-improvement.

Moreover, having a plot armor doesn't mean that you become complacent or passive in the face of challenges. It doesn't mean that you sit back and wait for things to magically work out. It means that you take proactive steps to navigate through challenges with resilience, determination, and a positive mindset. You become the hero of your own story, taking charge of your life and making decisions that align with your desired outcome.

Just like a skilled author carefully crafts the plot armor for their characters, you too can consciously create and strengthen your plot armor in your own life story. Here are some practical steps you can take to enhance your belief in your plot armor and make it invincible:

Cultivate a Positive Mindset: Your mindset plays a crucial role in shaping your reality. Choose to adopt a positive mindset that focuses on possibilities, solutions, and growth. Train your mind to see challenges as opportunities for learning and improvement rather than as threats. Surround yourself with positive influences, practice gratitude, and affirm yourself with empowering beliefs.

Set Clear Intentions: Be clear about what you want to achieve in your life and set intentions that align with your desires. Write down your goals, visualize yourself achieving them, and take inspired action towards them. When you have a clear sense of purpose and direction, you strengthen your plot armor by giving it a solid foundation to build upon.

Trust Your Inner Wisdom: You possess an innate wisdom within you that knows what's best for you. Learn to trust your intuition and inner guidance. Listen to your gut instincts, pay attention to synchronicities, and trust that the universe is always conspiring in your favor. When you trust your inner wisdom, you strengthen your plot armor by tapping into a higher power that guides and protects you.

Embrace Resilience: Resilience is the ability to bounce back from challenges and setbacks. Embrace resilience as a key quality of your plot armor. Instead of getting discouraged by failures or setbacks, see them as opportunities to learn, grow, and come back even stronger. Cultivate resilience by developing coping skills, practicing self-care, and surrounding yourself with a supportive network.

Practice Visualization: Just like an author visualizes the desired outcome for their characters, practice visualizing yourself as the hero of your own story. See yourself overcoming challenges, achieving your goals, and emerging victorious. Use all your senses to create a vivid mental picture of your desired reality. The more you visualize yourself with an invincible plot armor, the more you reinforce that belief in your subconscious mind.

Take Inspired Action: Your plot armor doesn't mean that you sit back and wait for things to happen. It means that you take inspired action towards your goals, trusting that your plot armor will guide and protect you along the way. Be proactive in taking steps that align with your intentions, and keep moving forward with determination and perseverance.

Surround Yourself with Supportive People: Just like the protagonist in a story often has a supporting cast of characters, surround yourself with people who believe in you, support your dreams, and uplift your spirits. Avoid negative influences or toxic relationships that drain your energy or dampen your belief in your plot armor. Surrounding yourself with positive and supportive people strengthens your plot armor by creating a supportive environment.

In conclusion, just as a plot armor protects the hero of a story from all adversaries, challenges, and obstacles, you too have a plot armor in your own life story. It is an unbreakable shield that safeguards you from harm, guides you through challenges, and empowers you to emerge as a stronger and better version of yourself. By cultivating a positive mindset, setting clear intentions, trusting your inner wisdom, embracing resilience, practicing visualization, taking inspired action, and surrounding yourself with supportive people, you can reinforce your belief in your plot armor and make it invincible. Remember, you are the director and author of your own life story, and with an unwavering belief in your plot armor, you can overcome any challenge, achieve your dreams, and create a life of success and fulfillment. Trust in your plot armor, and let it be your unbreakable shield

Chapter 9. Affirmations and Positive Self-Talk

A. What are Affirmations and Positive Self-Talk?

Affirmations and positive self-talk are powerful tools for shaping your thoughts and beliefs. Affirmations are positive statements that you repeat to yourself, usually about a specific goal or desire. Positive self-talk refers to the inner dialogue that you have with yourself on a daily basis. Both affirmations and positive self-talk are designed to help you focus on your goals and reinforce positive beliefs and attitudes.

B. How to Use Affirmations and Positive Self-Talk

Identify your goals and desires: Begin by identifying your goals and desires. What do you want to achieve in your life? What are your core values and beliefs?

Create positive affirmations: Create affirmations that align with your goals and desires. Make sure that the affirmations are in the present tense and focus on what you want to achieve, rather than what you don't want.

Repeat your affirmations daily: Repeat your affirmations to yourself several times a day, either out loud or silently in your mind. Repeat them when you wake up, before you go to sleep, and throughout the day.

Practice positive self-talk: Pay attention to the inner dialogue that you have with yourself and make a conscious effort to replace negative self-talk with positive self-talk. Reframe negative thoughts and beliefs into positive, empowering statements.

Feelings: attached feelings to your affirmations whenever you speak or repeat your information always ensure to have the maximum amount of feelings and beliefs attached to them when you speak so you need to repeat these affirmations with the deepest possible feelings feel it in your heart feel it in your mind your soul you need to feel what you're saying and believe in what you're saying and if you have the strong belief and faith in what you are repeating over and over again and believe that it has already happened in that case you will manifest it and you will definitely get what you want. In the beginning it will sound fake but keep doing it and slowly it will feel natural to you.

You can take your phone and start recording an audio on your phone for the information. So you can record your information and once they are recorded you can play them within the 90 minutes off the time that you go to. For the first 90 minutes your brain is still active and it can listen to anything that is being said so if you're playing this within the first 90 minutes of your sleep in that case you will be able to hear it and your subconscious mind will be able to hear what you're saying so you can repeat your information in your sleep and they will be recorded by your subconscious mind and will help you in the manifestation process.

C. The Benefits of Affirmations and Positive Self-Talk

Improved focus and motivation: By focusing on your goals and desires through affirmations and positive self-talk, you can increase your focus and motivation towards achieving your goals.

Increased self-confidence: By repeating positive affirmations and practicing positive self-talk, you can increase your self-confidence and self-belief, making it easier to take action towards your goals.

Improved mental health: Affirmations and positive self-talk can help to reduce stress and anxiety, improving your overall mental health and well-being.

Shifted mindset: Regular affirmations and positive self-talk can help to shift your mindset and beliefs, making it easier to manifest your desires and achieve your goals.

D. Conclusion

Affirmations and positive self-talk are powerful tools for shaping your thoughts and beliefs, and can help you to focus on your goals and achieve your desires. Make affirmations and positive self-talk a daily habit and watch as your life changes for the better. Remember, the words you speak to yourself have the power to shape your reality, so make sure that you are speaking words of positivity, empowerment, and success.

Chapter 10. Crafting Powerful Affirmations for Wealth and Success

A. What are Affirmations for Wealth and Success?

Affirmations for wealth and success are specific, positive statements that you repeat to yourself, designed to help you attract more wealth and success into your life. These affirmations help to focus your thoughts and beliefs on your financial goals and desires, allowing you to manifest abundance and prosperity in your life.

B. How to Craft Powerful Affirmations for Wealth and Success

Identify your financial goals and desires: Begin by identifying your financial goals and desires. What do you want to achieve in terms of wealth and success? What is your definition of financial freedom?

Make affirmations specific and personal: Craft affirmations that are specific to your financial goals and desires. Make sure that the affirmations are written in the present tense and focus on what you have, rather than what you don't have.

Use positive, empowering language: Use positive, empowering language in your affirmations. Avoid negative words such as "don't," "can't," or "won't." Instead, use words such as "I am," "I have," and "I will."

Repeat your affirmations daily: Repeat your affirmations to yourself several times a day, either out loud or silently in your mind. Repeat them when you wake up, before you go to sleep, and throughout the day.

C. Examples of Affirmations for Wealth and Success

"I am attracting abundance and prosperity into my life."

"I am a successful and wealthy person."

"I am capable of generating unlimited wealth."

"I am deserving of financial freedom and success."

"I have a successful and thriving business."

D. The Benefits of Affirmations for Wealth and Success

Improved focus and motivation: By focusing on your financial goals and desires through affirmations, you can increase your focus and motivation towards achieving financial success.

Increased self-confidence: By repeating positive affirmations about wealth and success, you can increase your self-confidence and self-belief, making it easier to take action towards your financial goals.

Shifted mindset: Regular affirmations for wealth and success can help to shift your mindset and beliefs, making it easier to manifest abundance and prosperity in your life.

Attraction of wealth and success: By repeating affirmations for wealth and success, you can attract more wealth and success into your life, allowing you to achieve your financial goals and desires.

E. Conclusion

Affirmations for wealth and success are powerful tools for shaping your thoughts and beliefs about your financial future. Make affirmations for wealth and success a daily habit and watch as your financial situation improves. Remember, the words you speak to yourself have the power to shape your financial reality, so make sure that you are speaking words of abundance, prosperity, and success.

Chapter 11. Implementing Affirmations into Your Daily Routine

A. Understanding the Power of Daily Affirmations

Daily affirmations have the power to shape your thoughts, beliefs, and actions, allowing you to attract more wealth and success into your life. By repeating affirmations for wealth and success regularly, you can train your brain to focus on your financial goals and desires, making it easier to manifest abundance and prosperity.

B. Incorporating Affirmations into Your Daily Routine

Make affirmations a morning ritual: Start your day with affirmations for wealth and success. Repeat them to yourself when you first wake up, before you begin your day.

Repeat affirmations throughout the day: Repeat your affirmations to yourself throughout the day, either out loud or silently in your mind. Repeat them when you feel stressed or anxious, when you're stuck in traffic, or when you're waiting in line.

Use affirmations as a form of self-talk: Use affirmations as a form of positive self-talk. Instead of speaking negative thoughts to yourself, speak positive affirmations for wealth and success.

Write affirmations down: Write your affirmations down and place them in areas where you'll see them often, such as your office or car. This will help to reinforce your affirmations and keep your financial goals and desires top of mind.

C. The Benefits of Daily Affirmations

Improved focus and motivation: By focusing on your financial goals and desires through daily affirmations, you can increase your focus and motivation towards achieving financial success.

Increased self-confidence: By repeating positive affirmations for wealth and success on a daily basis, you can increase your self-confidence and self-belief, making it easier to take action towards your financial goals.

Shifted mindset: Daily affirmations for wealth and success can help to shift your mindset and beliefs, making it easier to manifest abundance and prosperity in your life.

Attraction of wealth and success: By repeating affirmations for wealth and success daily, you can attract more wealth and success into your life, allowing you to achieve your financial goals and desires.

D. Conclusion

Incorporating affirmations into your daily routine is a simple, yet powerful way to attract more wealth and success into your life. Make affirmations for wealth and success a daily habit and watch as your financial situation improves. Remember, the words you speak to yourself have the power to shape your financial reality, so make sure that you are speaking words of abundance, prosperity, and success.

E. The Power of Affirmations: How One Man Changed His Life

James had always been the black sheep of his family. He struggled to excel in school and couldn't land a good job like his friends. He lived with his parents well into his thirties, scraping by on meager paychecks. His self-esteem was at an all-time low, and he felt like a failure. But one day, he stumbled upon the law of attraction and the power of affirmations. He started working on creating the perfect affirmation for himself, one that would help him achieve his dreams of becoming a successful business owner, owning a house, and finding a partner.

Every night before going to bed, John repeated his affirmation in his mind, visualizing himself as the successful owner of a profitable business with many employees. He also imagined himself owning a beautiful house and being married to a loving partner. He did this for several weeks without seeing any results, but he kept going, trusting that the universe would bring him what he desired.

One day, things started to change. James's boss at work noticed his positive attitude and work ethic, and he was given a promotion. The extra income allowed him to save up enough money to start his own business. He took the leap of faith, and his business started to flourish from the very beginning. He couldn't believe how quickly things were falling into place.

As his business grew, James was able to buy his own house and even found a girlfriend who shared his passions and values. They fell in love and got married, and James finally felt like his life was complete. He was no longer the black sheep of his family. He had earned the respect of his peers and was a successful business owner.

All of this was possible because of the power of affirmations. By focusing his mind on what he wanted to achieve and believing that it was possible, James was able to attract success and abundance into his life. He had finally discovered his true potential and was living the life he had always dreamed of.

Chapter 12. Goal Setting and Action Planning

A. Understanding the Importance of Goal Setting

Goal setting is an essential aspect of the law of attraction, as it helps you to focus your thoughts, beliefs, and actions towards your financial goals and desires. When you set clear and specific financial goals, you give your subconscious mind a clear direction to work towards, making it easier to attract wealth and success into your life.

B. Steps to Setting Effective Financial Goals

Be specific: Set specific, measurable financial goals that are realistic and achievable. For example, instead of saying "I want to be rich," say "I want to have $1 million in savings by the end of the year."

Make them time-bound: Set a deadline for each financial goal. This will help to give you a sense of urgency and motivation to achieve your goals.

Write them down: Write down your financial goals and place them in areas where you'll see them often, such as your office or car. This will help to reinforce your goals and keep them top of mind.

Prioritize: Prioritize your financial goals and focus on the most important ones first.

C. Action Planning

Break down goals into smaller steps: Once you have set your financial goals, break them down into smaller, achievable steps. This will help to make your goals seem less overwhelming and more manageable.

Create an action plan: Write down a plan of action for each goal, including the specific steps you need to take, the resources you need, and a timeline for achieving each step.

Take action: Take consistent, daily action towards your financial goals. Focus on taking one step at a time and don't get discouraged if you don't see immediate results.

Track progress: Track your progress and celebrate your achievements along the way. This will help to keep you motivated and focused on your financial goals.

D. Conclusion

Goal setting and action planning are crucial aspects of the law of attraction, allowing you to focus your thoughts, beliefs, and actions towards your financial goals and desires. By setting specific, achievable financial goals and taking consistent, daily action towards them, you can attract more wealth and success into your life and achieve financial freedom.

Chapter 13. The Importance of Having Specific, Measurable Goals

A. Why Specificity Matters

The law of attraction states that what you focus on expands, so it is important to be as specific as possible when setting your financial goals. Specific, measurable goals give you a clear direction to work towards and help you to focus your thoughts, beliefs, and actions towards attracting wealth and success into your life.

B. The Benefits of Measurable Goals

Clarity: Measurable goals provide clarity and a sense of direction, making it easier for you to stay focused on what you want to achieve.

Motivation: Measurable goals help to increase motivation and drive as you see progress towards your financial goals.

Tracking progress: Measurable goals make it easier to track your progress and make adjustments along the way.

Improved performance: Having measurable goals helps you to perform better, as you have a clear idea of what you need to achieve and what you need to do to get there.

C. How to Set Specific, Measurable Financial Goals

Be specific: Be as specific as possible when setting your financial goals. For example, instead of saying "I want to be rich," say "I want to have $1 million in savings by the end of the year."

Make them measurable: Make your financial goals measurable, so you can track your progress and see how close you are to achieving them.

Set deadlines: Set deadlines for each financial goal, so you have a sense of urgency and motivation to achieve your goals.

D. Conclusion

Having specific, measurable financial goals is an essential aspect of the law of attraction, as it helps you to focus your thoughts, beliefs, and actions towards attracting wealth and success into your life. By setting clear and specific goals, you can increase your motivation and drive, improve your performance, and track your progress towards achieving financial freedom.

E. Writing Your Goals Down

A. The Power of Writing Your Goals

Writing down your financial goals has been shown to increase the likelihood of achieving them. This is because writing your goals down helps to make them more concrete and tangible, as well as helping you to focus your thoughts and take your goals seriously.

B. The Benefits of Writing Your Goals Down

Increased clarity: Writing your goals down helps you to clarify what you really want and what is most important to you.

Improved focus: Writing your goals down helps to focus your thoughts and keep you on track towards achieving your financial goals.

Increased motivation: Writing your goals down can help to increase motivation and drive, as you can see what you need to do to achieve your goals.

Better memory: Writing your goals down helps you to remember what you want to achieve, which is important when trying to attract wealth and success into your life.

C. How to Write Your Goals Down

Choose a format: Choose a format that works best for you, whether it be a journal, notebook, or computer file.

Be specific: Be as specific as possible when writing your financial goals, making sure to include dates, amounts, and other specific details.

Use positive language: Use positive language when writing your goals, as this will help to attract positive energy into your life.

Review regularly: Review your written financial goals regularly, making sure to adjust them as needed to keep them in line with your changing circumstances and priorities.

D. Conclusion

Writing down your financial goals is an important aspect of the law of attraction, as it helps you to clarify what you really want, focus your thoughts, and increase motivation and drive towards achieving financial success. By taking the time to write your financial goals down, you can increase the likelihood of achieving them and bring your dreams of wealth and success into reality.

F. Taking Action to Achieve Your Goals

A. The Importance of Taking Action

Thinking positively and visualizing your goals is only half the battle in attracting wealth and success into your life. To truly achieve your financial goals, it is essential to take action and make things happen.

B. How to Take Action

Make a plan: Make a plan of action, breaking down your financial goals into smaller, more manageable steps.

Take consistent, deliberate action: Take consistent, deliberate action towards your financial goals, no matter how small the steps may be.

Surround yourself with positive influences: Surround yourself with positive influences, such as successful people and supportive friends and family.

Believe in yourself: Believe in yourself and your abilities, and don't let self-doubt hold you back.

C. Overcoming Obstacles

Anticipate challenges: Anticipate challenges and obstacles that may arise, and have a plan in place to overcome them.

Be persistent: Be persistent in your efforts towards your financial goals, even when obstacles arise.

Learn from failures: Learn from failures and use them as opportunities for growth and learning.

D. Conclusion

Taking action towards your financial goals is an essential part of the law of attraction, and it is what separates those who succeed from those who don't. By taking consistent, deliberate action, believing in yourself, and overcoming obstacles, you can attract wealth and success into your life and make your financial dreams a reality.

Creating My Destiny: How Visualization Helped Me Achieve My Dream Job

One day, while I was working in New Jersey, a friend of mine who also worked at the same company called me. He excitedly told me that he had been working as a contractor for HP at a company called Campus, and they had an opening that he thought I would be a perfect fit for. He mentioned that the pay rate was higher than what I was currently making, and he would also receive a referral bonus for bringing me on board. After giving it some thought, I decided to take a chance and explore this opportunity.

I went through the interview process and was thrilled when I received the news that I had been selected for the position. Saying goodbye to my boss and colleagues in New

Jersey, I packed my bags and moved with my family to Michigan, to a small town called Kalamazoo. It was a big decision for us, as we had many friends and were comfortable in New Jersey, but the potential increase in pay was too tempting to pass up.

There was one catch though - the company would not sponsor me for an H-1B visa, and I had recently obtained an Employment Authorization Document (EAD) which allowed me to work for any employer. This meant that if my green card application were to face any setbacks and not get approved, I could be in trouble. Despite this risk, I decided to take a leap of faith and join the company on my EAD directly, instead of continuing on my H-1B, which was not a recommended approach according to online forums that I used to follow for immigration-related topics.

What kept me going was my unwavering faith in the universe and the belief that everything would work out for the best. I was confident that I would eventually get my green card when the time was right, and I was willing to take the risk. It was a leap of faith, and I had already taken the plunge, trusting that the universe and the higher power would not let me down.

We embarked on a new chapter of our lives with eager anticipation and a sense of adventure as we sold off all our furniture and belongings that were too large to fit in our minivan. We carefully chose only the essential furniture, such as beds and a dining table, which we entrusted to a mover to transport to our new home in Michigan. As for the rest, we packed our minivan to the brim with our cooking utensils, spices, bags of clothes, TV, and other necessary items. Anything that we couldn't take with us, we gave away to neighbors, friends, and family, or simply discarded in the garbage dumpster.

It was a thrilling but challenging time as we prepared to start a new life in Michigan. We were aware of the frigid weather in this region, even colder than New Jersey, and we didn't know many people, except for one friend who promised to introduce us to others. Despite having a young daughter, we were determined to face these challenges head-on and emerge victorious on the other side.

I remember the night we packed everything and handed over our belongings to the mover in the afternoon. We loaded up the van at night and set off on our journey from New Jersey to Michigan on a Monday. Just a few days earlier, I had signed off from my existing job, and Saturday and Sunday were spent packing. We drove through the night, hoping to reach our destination in the morning and head straight to the office.

However, it was snowing heavily that night, and we hadn't equipped our tires for the wintry roads. To make matters worse, our GPS was outdated, with maps that were several years old. Despite these challenges, we managed to find the main road and relied on our friend's directions to locate our destination in the newly-built community. We followed any large vehicle we could find on the road to stay safe in the dark and snowy conditions.

Finally, we arrived at our friend's place late at night, only to find that he had gone to sleep and was not responding to our knocks on his door. The area was covered in thick snow, and the temperature was well below freezing. With our daughter getting restless in the car, we waited for a while and rang the doorbell multiple times to no avail. I decided to venture around the building and check the back window of his apartment. Wading through knee-deep snow, I called out his name, and he eventually woke up and came to the front to hand me the keys.

We opened the apartment to find that there was no furniture or bed, just a bare carpet. However, the heat was on, and it wasn't too cold. We improvised by laying down some comforters for our daughter to sleep in the bedroom. As for ourselves, we made do with a couple of comforters on the floor and spent the night as best as we could.

The next morning, I went to the office to start my new job. I was responsible for technical support, managing the ticketing system for HP and their client, Delphi Auto Parts, which had factories all around the world. My team and I handled password resets, Windows server management, and other related tasks. Despite the initial challenges, things started to fall into place as we made friends with other Indian families who were also working in the same company. We formed a close-knit group, and we would gather at someone's house every Saturday for a small party and get-together.

Every evening, after a long day at work, I would come back home to find my daughter feeling bored and restless. The harsh cold and freezing weather outside made it difficult for her to go out and play, and she didn't have any friends in our new neighborhood yet. The weekends were the only time when we could go to someone's home and she could meet a few kids, but that was not enough to keep her entertained throughout the week.

To add some excitement to her evenings, me and my wife started taking her to a nearby McDonald's that had a kids play area. We would order a kids meal for her, which came with a small toy that she would eagerly anticipate. As soon as we entered, her eyes would light up with joy as she spotted the colorful play area. It had tunnels, slides, and steps that she would navigate with enthusiasm, giggling and laughing as she played.

We would sit at a nearby table, sipping on a hot cup of coffee, and watching our daughter have a blast in the play area. She would make new friends, often other kids who were also looking for some indoor entertainment during the cold weather. They would run, climb, and slide together, creating their own little adventures in the play area. It was heartwarming to see our daughter's face light up with happiness as she formed new connections and had fun.

The McDonald's play area became a regular part of our routine. It was a place where our daughter could burn off her energy, make friends, and have some much-needed social interaction. It also provided us with a moment of respite, where we could relax and enjoy a brief moment together while keeping an eye on our daughter.

Despite the cold and freezing weather outside, the warmth and laughter inside the McDonald's play area brought a sense of joy to our evenings. It became a special place for our daughter, where she could forget about the weather and the lack of friends in our neighborhood, and simply be a carefree kid. The small toy that came with the kids meal also became a cherished item for her, and she would excitedly show it off to us and her friends.

Looking back, those evenings spent at the McDonald's play area were not just about the entertainment it provided for my daughter, but also the precious memories we created together. It was a reminder of how even in the midst of challenges, we can find joy and connection in unexpected places. It taught us the value of making the best out of every situation and finding silver linings, even on the coldest and most challenging days.

In a few short days, the routine of going to the same McDonald's every evening started to lose its appeal. My wife and I realized that we needed a change, and she suggested going to India to stay with her mom for a while. She thought our daughter, Tina, would enjoy the company of her cousins and other kids in the building, and it would be a good break for all of us. With the prospect of Tina having more kids to play with and the busy atmosphere of India, we decided it was worth a shot. It would also be summertime in India, unlike the cold spring weather we were experiencing in Michigan.

So, my wife and Tina went to India, and I stayed back to continue working. But fate had other plans for me. One day, we were called into a meeting by the Senior Management, and to our shock, we were told that the project was over and everyone was being let go. It had only been three months since I started working on the project, and we hadn't saved much money from our short time there. We were asked to pack up and not return to our desks. It was a surreal experience, as we were escorted to our desks to collect our personal belongings in front of our supervisor, but we were not allowed to touch the computers. It was a stark reminder of how uncertain life can be.

With the India trip already depleting our savings, including the expensive round-trip tickets, which cost around $1500 per person, and additional expenses that would need to be covered while my wife and daughter were there, I was left in a tough spot. We had come to Michigan for only three months with just three months' pay, and now I had lost my job. I was worried about how we would continue paying the monthly rent for our apartment, as I had signed a year-long lease. Finding another job became my top priority, but the situation seemed daunting.

Despite the challenges, I remained hopeful and determined to turn things around for my family. It was a difficult time, but I knew that I had to keep moving forward and find a new source of income. Little did I know that this setback would eventually lead to unforeseen opportunities and shape our lives in unexpected ways. But for now, my focus was on finding another job to keep our heads above water and ensure that we could continue to support ourselves in the midst of uncertainty.

As I delved deeper into the principles of the law of attraction, I became more determined than ever to manifest the job of my dreams. I diligently followed all the recommended steps, leaving no stone unturned. I updated my resume with utmost care, making sure it reflected my skills and experience in the best possible light. I posted it on various job portals, eagerly anticipating the flood of responses that would surely come my way.

But I didn't stop there. I understood that visualization was a powerful tool in the manifestation process, so I began to regularly visualize myself in my ideal job. I would close my eyes and imagine sitting in a comfortable chair in a modern cubicle, facing a computer screen with confidence and enthusiasm. I would envision a colleague coming up to me with a smile, congratulating me on a job well done, and I would graciously accept their praise with a thank you and a firm handshake. These vivid visualizations fueled my motivation and kept me focused on my goal.

I also knew that preparation was key to success, so I meticulously researched and prepared for potential interview questions. I compiled a list of common interview questions and answers, memorized them, and practiced delivering them with poise and confidence in front of the mirror. I made it a priority to stay updated with the latest industry trends and news, constantly improving my knowledge and skills to stay ahead of the competition. I updated my resume multiple times, ensuring that it was always tailored to the specific requirements of each job application.

Despite my efforts, days passed by without any concrete results. I received calls from numerous recruiters, and I went through several initial interviews, but nothing seemed to materialize. Internal anxiety threatened to creep in, but I refused to let doubt take hold. I consciously replaced any negative thoughts with unwavering faith that I would find a job quickly, one that paid even more than my previous position. I reminded myself that this was just a temporary setback, and that the universe was working in my favor, guiding me towards my true desires.

One day, I received a call from a recruiter who informed me of an urgent requirement at Washington Mutual Bank (WAMU) for a server admin position. As I listened to the job description, I realized that I was a perfect fit for the role, with my skills and MCSE certification aligning perfectly with the requirements. I wasted no time in sending my resume to the recruiter, feeling a surge of excitement and hope. I couldn't help but visualize myself in that role, performing my duties with expertise and satisfaction, surrounded by happy colleagues and supervisors who praised my work.

Looking back, I realized that losing my previous job had actually been a blessing in disguise. It had led me to this opportunity at WAMU, which seemed like the perfect fit for me and my family. My daughter's comfort and happiness were a priority for me, and this job seemed to offer the ideal location for us. I now understood that the universe had answered my prayers in a way that I couldn't have anticipated. It was a reminder for me to trust the process, have unwavering faith, and keep visualizing my desired outcome with absolute certainty.

With renewed determination, I eagerly awaited a positive response from the recruiter, ready to take on this new opportunity with gusto and gratitude. I was grateful for the journey that had brought me to this point and confident that my continued faith and perseverance would lead me to the job of my dreams. I was ready to step into my new role as a server admin at WAMU, fully prepared and equipped to excel in my responsibilities and create a fulfilling career for myself.

The recruiter's email arrived in my inbox, and my heart skipped a beat. It was the opportunity I had been waiting for - the chance to be represented by someone who could potentially land me a job at the prestigious WAMU company. With bated breath, I replied back, confirming my acceptance of the rate and expressing my eagerness for the recruiter to represent me to the company.

Days went by, and I was on pins and needles, anxiously waiting for the interview call. The recruiter had assured me that the call could happen anytime in the next day or two, and I was constantly checking my phone and email for any updates. But the call never came. The next day passed, and then the third day, without any word from the recruiter.

Feeling restless and disappointed, I finally took matters into my own hands and called the recruiter to inquire about the status of the job requirement. To my dismay, the recruiter informed me that the position had been filled, and my resume was not selected. However, he assured me that he would keep my resume on file and notify me if any other openings came up in the future. It was a blow to my hopes, but I tried to keep my spirits up.

I couldn't help but feel a sense of longing for the vision I had nurtured over the past few days. I had imagined myself sitting in a cubicle on the 17th floor of the WAMU building, near the glass window that overlooked the breathtaking city skyline of Seattle, Washington. It was a vivid image that had captured my imagination, and I couldn't let go of the dream.

Unable to contain my curiosity, I turned to Google Maps to find the location of the WAMU building. I couldn't print the page, so I took a blank piece of paper and sketched a rough outline of the tower, marking the floor that I had imagined my cubicle to be on. It was a child-like drawing, but it helped me visualize my dream even more vividly.

I studied the skyline of Seattle, closing my eyes and trying to visualize the buildings, roads, and people from the height of the 17th floor. I could feel the excitement and happiness welling up inside me as I imagined myself sitting near the glass window, looking out at the bustling city below. It became a daily ritual for me - sitting quietly in my chair, motionless, closing my eyes, and immersing myself in the scene of my dream job at WAMU.

In my mind's eye, I could see someone coming up behind me, shaking my hand, and welcoming me to WAMU. The scene played out in my mind over and over again, and each time, I felt a surge of joy and gratitude towards God and the universe for helping me manifest my dream job.

I continued to visualize my dream job at WAMU several times a day, pouring all my energy and intention into it. It became a source of inspiration and motivation for me, keeping me focused and determined in my job search. Despite the initial setback, I refused to give up on my vision, holding onto the belief that it was only a matter of time before my dream became a reality. I remained grateful for the opportunity and hopeful for the future, trusting that the universe had something even better in store for me.

As the day passed, I couldn't help but keep visualizing the opportunity that might come my way. I had been eagerly waiting for a call, hoping that something positive would happen. Just when I least expected it, I received a call from a person named Suresh. He introduced himself as someone who worked for Cognizant and informed me that there was a requirement for a Server Admin position with WAMU. He asked if I was available and interested in the opportunity. I eagerly replied with a yes, recalling that I had received a call from Cognizant a few days back for an interview that never happened.

Suresh clarified that he hadn't called me before, but he found my resume on their portal. He mentioned that someone from their company, Cognition, might have put it there when I had applied for another position in WAMU, which was now closed. Nevertheless, he thought my resume matched the current requirement, and he wanted to know if I was interested. I was thrilled at the possibility and requested him to send me the job description.

Soon, Suresh shared the job description with me, and I realized that it was quite similar to the previous one, with the exception of the inclusion of Linux administration along with Windows. While I was confident in my skills as a Windows Server Administrator, I was not as proficient in Linux. I had some basic knowledge of Linux commands from my earlier experience with DOS and occasional use of Linux servers, but I had never formally studied or worked with Linux servers. I expressed my concerns to Suresh, stating that I couldn't assure him that I would be able to crack the interview due to my limited experience with Linux.

However, Suresh reassured me, saying not to worry about it. He suggested that I answer the Linux-related questions to the best of my knowledge and that if I got selected, it would be great, otherwise, they would continue to look for other suitable opportunities for me. I appreciated his support and agreed to give it a shot. I received the Right to Represent (RTR) form from him, which I promptly filled out and sent back.

The very next day, Suresh called me again to schedule the interview with the manager. He asked about my availability and when I could join, to which I responded with eagerness and a willingness to start as soon as possible. We finalized a time for the interview, and Suresh also mentioned that he had compiled a list of 10 questions that the other candidates had been asked in previous interviews for the same position. He thought it would be helpful for me to prepare for these questions as they might come up in my interview as well. He sent me the list, and I was thrilled to have them in hand. I had previously compiled a set of questions from my past interviews, so I added Suresh's questions to my list, making them my top priority. I created a separate Word document and diligently answered each question, elaborating on them with additional content that I gathered from thorough research on the internet. I made sure the language used was natural and conversational, rather than sounding like I was reading from a script. Once I finalized my answers, I practiced them repeatedly, eagerly waiting for the interview day.

In my mind, I was already visualizing myself succeeding in the interview and securing the job. I couldn't help but think about the potential increase in income compared to my previous job or the job from which I was recently laid off. I was determined to give it my all and make a strong impression during the interview, confident that this opportunity could be the turning point in my career.

The day of the interview had finally arrived, and I was determined to ace it. I had spent hours preparing, meticulously jotting down all the possible questions and their ideal answers in a word document. The document was extensive, spanning 8 to 10 pages and containing nearly 100 questions. While I couldn't memorize everything verbatim, I made sure to understand the concepts thoroughly and remember the key elements of each answer to the best of my ability.

To further hone my skills, I practiced in front of the mirror, imagining myself sitting in the 17th floor office of the WAMU building, overlooking the magnificent Seattle skyline. I could see the buildings, roads, cars, and people bustling about as I delivered my answers confidently, adding pauses, "umms," and "aaas" to make them sound more natural and spontaneous.

Finally, the moment arrived, and the interview commenced with the initial introductions. As the questions started, I was pleasantly surprised to find that the first question asked was identical to the one on my list. It was word-for-word, as if I was reading it from my sheet. I took a deep breath, composed myself, and delivered my well-prepared response, making sure to sound authentic and not like I was reading from somewhere.

The interviewers seemed impressed with my answers, and we proceeded to the next question, which again matched exactly with my second question on the sheet. I answered with confidence, and the pattern continued for the third, fourth, fifth, and all the way up to the tenth question. Not a single question was outside of the ones I had prepared for. The interviewers seemed pleased with my performance, and by the end of the interview, they practically confirmed that they would like to work with me.

As the call ended, I couldn't contain my excitement. It felt as if I had already secured the job. I wasn't surprised, though, because in my mind, I had already visualized myself working at WAMU on the 17th floor, with a breathtaking view of the Seattle skyline from my desk. Now, all that was left was to wait for their response, which they promised to provide within a day. Everyone around me was thrilled, and the anticipation was palpable. I eagerly awaited the confirmation of my dream job, where I could see the Seattle skyline from the 17th floor of the WAMU building.

After my interview, I anxiously awaited the outcome, knowing in my heart that I had attracted this job. I received a call from Suresh, who wanted to know how the interview went. He assured me that he would talk to my hiring manager on my behalf. Just an hour later, he called me back with the most amazing news - I had been selected for the job! I was overjoyed and filled with excitement, but not at all surprised. I knew that the universe had answered my prayers and granted my request.

I wasted no time in calling my wife to share the good news. Everyone in my family was thrilled for me. The next day, Suresh called again, this time to discuss the pay package. To my amazement, they offered me the highest pay package for this role, which was even more than what I was earning previously. Moreover, since Washington had no state tax, it was a double win for me in terms of savings. Without any hesitation, I gladly accepted the offer.

With everything falling into place, I packed my belongings and flew to Seattle, where I temporarily stayed in a hotel while searching for an apartment. I had limited savings and was eagerly anticipating my first paycheck, but I didn't want to waste any time in starting my new job on Monday as scheduled. I quickly found an apartment and made arrangements to move in soon. In the meantime, I stayed in the hotel, eagerly counting down the days until my job officially began.

The anticipation was palpable as I made my way to the address that Suresh had given me. It was in downtown Seattle, and I couldn't help but feel thrilled about the prospect of working in such a bustling and dynamic area. I had imagined a modern building with floor-to-ceiling glass windows offering panoramic views of the iconic Seattle skyline. However, as I entered the building and made my way to the second floor, I couldn't help but feel a bit disappointed. The environment was gloomy, with old cubicles that seemed out of place in the modern city.

Suresh led me to a cubicle and gestured for me to take a seat. I looked around, trying to spot the Seattle skyline, but all I could see were the windows at the edge of the hall. It was not the grand view I had imagined, and I couldn't help but feel a twinge of disappointment. However, I quickly reminded myself that I was grateful for the job opportunity at WAMU, even if the view didn't match my visualizations. After all, not everything in life turns out exactly as we imagine it, and I was still thankful for the job I had attracted.

Suresh then mentioned that we needed to go to the next building to collect my laptop. I was curious about why we needed to go to a different building, and he explained that the next building was where the employees of WAMU, including my manager, Greg Seaberg, were located. He further clarified that as contractors, we sat in a separate building with other contractors. I nodded in understanding and followed him to the next building, brimming with curiosity about meeting my manager and starting my new job.

As we made our way to the other building, I couldn't help but reflect on how different things were from what I had initially imagined. Nevertheless, I remained optimistic and grateful for the opportunity to work at WAMU, with a higher income and better weather than Michigan. My family would soon join me, and I was determined to make the most of this new chapter in my life, despite the differences between my visualizations and reality.

As I walked alongside Suresh, we made our way down the building and towards the end of the block. Seattle, with its numerous slopes and hills reminiscent of San Francisco, presented a unique topography to navigate. The city seemed to go up and down in a continuous rhythm as we made our way towards the downtown area, which sloped downward towards the sea. As we approached our destination, I couldn't contain my excitement as I saw the building that I had only seen on Google before - the WAMU building.

My visualization dreams were coming true one by one as I stood in front of the exact building that I had imagined. I silently thanked the universe for this incredible moment as I eagerly awaited for the pedestrian light to turn green so we could cross the street. As we stood there, I couldn't help but feel overwhelmed with gratitude that I was actually here, witnessing this moment unfold. Finally, the walking sign turned white, and we crossed the road, making our way into the building. Suresh, with his ID, led the way, and we entered the building, heading towards the elevators. I couldn't help but notice that the building had 22 floors, a significant number, as I nervously looked at the switchboard, unsure of where we were going.

Suresh, with a confident gesture, raised his hand and pressed a button on the switchboard. My heart skipped a beat as I saw the number 17, the exact floor I had visualized. I couldn't believe my luck as the elevator doors closed, and we began ascending to the 17th floor. The anticipation was palpable as the elevator doors opened, and we stepped out. Suresh led the way, and I followed closely behind, navigating through the aisles until we made a right turn towards the glass wall at the edge of the building.

My excitement reached its peak as I looked at the glass wall, exactly as I had visualized. Unlike the previous building I had visited, this one had an entire wall made of glass, offering a breathtaking view of the city below. We were greeted by Matt, another manager on our team, who informed us that Greg, my direct manager, would be joining us shortly. As we sat around, chatting with Matt, I couldn't help but feel a sense of belonging as he welcomed me to the team. Moments later, Greg arrived, and we exchanged handshakes, before he showed me to the cubicle right next to his.

Greg pointed to the laptop on the desk and informed me that it was mine to use. He provided me with a temporary password to log in, and I quickly reset it to create my own password. I saved the changes, and Suresh expressed his gratitude to Greg for his time, leaving me with a sense of excitement and anticipation for the new chapter ahead.

I couldn't contain my excitement as Greg led me to my cubicle. He gestured towards the laptop on the desk and the laptop bag next to it. I quickly closed the laptop and carefully put it in the bag, making sure everything was in place. I was eager to join Suresh and head back to the contractor's building, but Greg had different plans.

"Where are you going?" Greg asked, catching me off guard. I stumbled for an answer, unsure of what to say. I mumbled something about going back to the contractor's building, but Greg shook his head.

"No, you don't go there," he said firmly. "This is your cubicle. You need to sit here, next to me. I'm managing this team, and you'll be reporting to me."

Suresh looked surprised, and I could see the exclamation mark in his expression. He nodded at Greg, saying, "Okay, Greg. That's good." He then turned to me and said, "Okay, Tony. Please let me know if you need anything from me. You have my number. Call me if you need anything, and I'll see you later." With that, Suresh left, leaving me alone with Greg.

I sat down at my cubicle, feeling a mix of nervousness and excitement. I asked Greg to help me set up the laptop and other equipment, and he patiently guided me through the process. Once everything was in place, I looked up and noticed the glass wall next to my cubicle. The entire wall was made of glass, offering a breathtaking view of the city of Seattle.

I couldn't resist the urge to get up and walk towards the glass wall. As I stood there, I was awe-struck. From the left to the right, I could see the skyline of Seattle, with tall buildings reaching for the sky. In front of the skyline was the sea, with big ships and container loading and unloading cranes lining the shore. The sea was a mesmerizing shade of green, and the sky above was painted in shades of blue with fluffy white clouds. It was even more beautiful than I had visualized in my dreams, and I felt overwhelmed with gratitude that my dream was coming true in every detail.

I couldn't believe that I was now a part of that skyline, sitting in my cubicle with a view that was beyond my wildest imagination. I felt a sense of accomplishment and fulfillment that words couldn't describe. I was grateful to Greg for giving me this opportunity, and I was determined to work hard and make the most of it. As I sat down at my desk, I couldn't wipe the smile off my face. My heart was filled with joy, and I was ready to embark on this new chapter of my life, grateful for the manifestation of my dreams.

After experiencing the power of the law of attraction firsthand, my faith in its effectiveness was unwavering. I was filled with an unshakable belief that anything I could visualize, I could achieve. I immediately called my wife to share the incredible story of how my visualizations had come to life in my new job.

I vividly recounted to her how I had visualized every detail of the office I was sitting in when I was searching for a job, and how that exact same office had materialized before my eyes when I got the job. The glass walls that offered a breathtaking view of the Seattle Skyline, the colorful ships sailing in the distance, the bustling buildings and cars - every minute detail was just as I had visualized it in my mind's eye. I was in awe of the power of visualization and manifestation, as I had successfully brought my desires into reality.

Reflecting on the experience, I realized that manifesting my visualizations had not been a difficult task at all. It simply required sitting down and imagining a scene where I was the director of my own life, with the power to shape every situation and circumstance. I was in control, and I could decide what would happen. I could create a scene of my life that would make me truly happy, complete with all the characters and elements that were necessary, whether real or imagined.

I had learned that the key to effective visualization was to make the scenes as vivid and real as possible. I could feel the sensations, touch and interact with objects, and experience the emotions associated with my desires as if they were already real. The clearer my visions became with each repetition, the more the universe responded to my prayers, granting me exactly what I had asked for.

I had also come to understand that I didn't need to concern myself with the steps or processes to achieve my desires. My focus should solely be on the end result - the destination where I wanted to be in my life. I needed to visualize that destination in all its glory, with every detail and information, as if I had already arrived there.

If I desired to be a multi millionaire, I visualized myself as one. I could see myself looking successful, dressed in luxurious attire, driving fancy cars, living in a grand mansion with a sprawling backyard and an impressive front gate. I could imagine the staff that would work in my home - the house manager, the cooks, the cleaners, the organizers - all catering to my every need. I could envision the lifestyle of a Multi Millionaire, with all the privileges and perks that came with it.

But visualization wasn't limited to just material wealth. Some people might visualize becoming a renowned artist, a singer, a dancer, or a painter. Others might dream of becoming a successful businessman, a doctor, a lawyer, or any other profession that resonated with their aspirations. The beauty of visualization was that it could be tailored to suit individual desires and goals.

I encouraged everyone to take the time to truly understand what they wanted in life and to visualize it with utmost clarity and detail. I urged them to imagine themselves already having achieved their goals and to feel the emotions associated with that success. I emphasized that the power of visualization was immense and that it could truly help them manifest their dreams into reality.

As I concluded my story, I hoped that my experiences would inspire others to harness the power of visualization and achieve their own goals. The key was to believe in the law of attraction, to have unwavering faith in the power of visualization, and to take deliberate actions towards realizing their desires. With determination, focus, and belief, anyone could create the life they truly desired.

Chapter 14. Overcoming Limiting Beliefs and Obstacles

A. Understanding Limiting Beliefs

Limiting beliefs are negative thought patterns and beliefs that hold you back from achieving your full potential. These beliefs can be related to your financial situation, self-worth, and more.

B. Identifying Limiting Beliefs

Pay attention to negative self-talk: Pay attention to negative self-talk and identify any limiting beliefs that may be holding you back.

Journal your thoughts: Journal your thoughts and feelings to help identify any limiting beliefs that may be present.

C. Overcoming Limiting Beliefs

Replace negative thoughts with positive affirmations: Replace negative thoughts and limiting beliefs with positive affirmations and self-talk.

Surround yourself with positive influences: Surround yourself with positive influences, such as successful people and supportive friends and family.

Practice gratitude: Practice gratitude and focus on the positive aspects of your life, rather than dwelling on the negative.

D. Overcoming Obstacles

Anticipate challenges: Anticipate challenges and obstacles that may arise, and have a plan in place to overcome them.

Be persistent: Be persistent in your efforts towards your financial goals, even when obstacles arise.

Learn from failures: Learn from failures and use them as opportunities for growth and learning.

E. Conclusion

Overcoming limiting beliefs and obstacles is a key part of the law of attraction and achieving financial success. By identifying and overcoming limiting beliefs, being persistent in the face of obstacles, and practicing gratitude, you can attract wealth and success into your life and reach your financial goals.

Chapter 15. Understanding Limiting Beliefs and How They Hold You Back

A. Definition of Limiting Beliefs

Limiting beliefs are negative thought patterns and beliefs that hold you back from achieving your full potential. These beliefs can be related to your financial situation, self-worth, and more.

B. Examples of Limiting Beliefs

I will never be wealthy: This limiting belief can hold you back from taking the necessary steps towards financial success.

Money is the root of all evil: This belief can prevent you from seeing the positive aspects of wealth and pursuing financial success.

I am not worthy of wealth: This limiting belief can prevent you from taking the necessary steps towards financial success and can lead to feelings of low self-worth.

C. How Limiting Beliefs Hold You Back

Limit your potential: Limiting beliefs limit your potential and prevent you from taking the necessary steps towards financial success.

Create negative self-talk: Limiting beliefs create negative self-talk and can lead to feelings of low self-worth.

Prevent action: Limiting beliefs can prevent you from taking action towards your financial goals and attract wealth and success into your life.

D. Overcoming Limiting Beliefs

Replace negative thoughts with positive affirmations: Replace negative thoughts and limiting beliefs with positive affirmations and self-talk.

Surround yourself with positive influences: Surround yourself with positive influences, such as successful people and supportive friends and family.

Practice gratitude: Practice gratitude and focus on the positive aspects of your life, rather than dwelling on the negative.

E. Conclusion

Understanding limiting beliefs and how they hold you back is an important part of the law of attraction and achieving financial success. By identifying and overcoming limiting beliefs, you can attract wealth and success into your life and reach your financial goals. By focusing on positive self-talk, surrounding yourself with positive influences, and practicing gratitude, you can develop a more positive and successful mindset.

Chapter 16. Strategies for Overcoming Limiting Beliefs

A. Identify Limiting Beliefs

The first step in overcoming limiting beliefs is to identify them. Ask yourself what negative thoughts and beliefs are holding you back and write them down. This will help you understand what you need to work on.

B. Reframe Limiting Beliefs

Once you have identified your limiting beliefs, reframe them. For example, if you believe that "money is the root of all evil," reframe it to "money is a tool that can be used for good."

C. Challenge Limiting Beliefs

Challenge your limiting beliefs by asking yourself if they are really true. Can you think of examples in your life or in the lives of others that contradict your limiting beliefs? This will help you see that your limiting beliefs are not absolute truths.

D. Surround Yourself with Positive Influences

Surround yourself with positive influences, such as successful people, supportive friends and family, and positive books and media. This will help you develop a positive and successful mindset.

E. Practice Positive Self-Talk

Practice positive self-talk by repeating positive affirmations to yourself each day. This will help you internalize positive beliefs and overcome negative thoughts and limiting beliefs.

F. Focus on Your Strengths and Accomplishments

Focus on your strengths and accomplishments, rather than your limitations and failures. This will help you build confidence and self-worth, and overcome limiting beliefs related to self-worth.

G. Seek Professional Help

If you are struggling to overcome limiting beliefs on your own, consider seeking professional help. A therapist or coach can help you identify and overcome limiting beliefs and develop a positive and successful mindset.

H. Conclusion

Overcoming limiting beliefs is an important part of the law of attraction and achieving financial success. By using the strategies outlined above, you can identify and overcome limiting beliefs and attract wealth and success into your life. Remember that changing negative thought patterns takes time and patience, but with persistence and determination, you can develop a positive and successful mindset.

Chapter 17. Dealing with Obstacles and Setbacks

A. Recognize Obstacles and Setbacks as Opportunities

It is important to recognize obstacles and setbacks as opportunities for growth and learning. Instead of seeing them as failures, view them as challenges that will help you become stronger and more resilient.

B. Stay Positive

Maintain a positive attitude even when faced with obstacles and setbacks. Remember that setbacks are temporary and that you have the power to overcome them.

C. Stay Focused on Your Goals

Stay focused on your goals, even when faced with obstacles and setbacks. Remember why you set your goals and what you hope to achieve. This will help you stay motivated and stay on track.

D. Find Solutions

Instead of dwelling on the problem, focus on finding solutions. Ask yourself what you can do to overcome the obstacle or setback, and take action.

E. Seek Support

Seek support from friends, family, or a coach if you need help overcoming an obstacle or setback. Having someone to talk to can help you stay positive and motivated.

F. Learn from Your Mistakes

Learn from your mistakes and use what you have learned to improve in the future. This will help you avoid similar obstacles and setbacks in the future.

G. Stay Committed to Your Goals

Stay committed to your goals, even when faced with obstacles and setbacks. Remember that setbacks are a natural part of the journey to success, and that you have the power to overcome them.

H. Conclusion

Obstacles and setbacks are a natural part of the journey to success. By staying positive, focused, and committed to your goals, you can overcome obstacles and setbacks and achieve your financial goals. Remember to see obstacles and setbacks as opportunities for growth and learning, and to stay motivated and focused on your goals.

Chapter 18. From Illness to Wellness: The Law of Attraction's Healing Potential to Achieve Optimal Health.

By now, you already know the incredible power of the Law of Attraction that can be used to manifest abundance and success in all areas of life. You know that by focusing your thoughts and beliefs on positive outcomes, you can manifest the life of your dreams. But did you know that this same power can also be applied to your health? That's right - the Law of Attraction can help you not only attract wealth, but also create miracles for your physical and mental wellbeing. Your thoughts and beliefs have a profound effect on your physical well-being, and by harnessing the power of the Law of Attraction, you can create miracles for your health.

Many of us struggle with health issues at some point in our lives. We may experience chronic pain, illness, disease, or simply a general feeling of unwellness. These challenges can be overwhelming, and it's easy to feel powerless in the face of medical diagnoses and treatments. But the truth is that we are not as powerless as we may think. Our thoughts and beliefs have a profound impact on our bodies, and by harnessing the power of the Law of Attraction, we can actually promote healing and wellbeing.

To start, it's crucial to recognize the connection between our thoughts, emotions, and physical well-being. Negative thoughts and emotions can affect our physical health, whereas positive ones can promote healing and wellness. This is because our thoughts and emotions emit a vibrational frequency that can impact our cells and organs. Our bodies are constantly vibrating, just like everything else in the universe. When our vibration is low, we may experience physical symptoms and illness. However, when our vibration is high, we feel energetic and healthy. The Law of Attraction emphasizes that we attract what we vibrate, which means that negative emotions like stress, fear, and anger generate lower frequencies that can disrupt the energy flow in our bodies and cause physical and emotional imbalances. These imbalances can lead to various health issues, from mild fatigue to chronic diseases like cancer and heart disease. Conversely, positive emotions like gratitude, love, and joy generate higher frequencies that promote healing and rejuvenation in our bodies. When we concentrate on positive thoughts and emotions, we can align our energy field with that of the universe, and in doing so, attract good health and vitality.

So, how can we use this knowledge to promote health and healing? With this in mind, it's easy to see how the Law of Attraction can be used to improve your health. The first step is to cultivate positive thoughts and beliefs about our bodies and our health. By focusing on positive thoughts and emotions, you can create a vibrational frequency that attracts health and vitality. This can be challenging, especially if we have been struggling with health issues for a long time. But remember, the Law of Attraction works with what we focus on, so if we continue to focus on our illness or pain, we will only attract more of the same. Instead, we must shift our focus to thoughts of health and wellbeing. This means letting go of negative beliefs and emotions that may be holding you back, and instead, focusing on what you want to create in your life.

Visualization: Visualization is an effective technique for using the Law of Attraction to improve your health. By visualizing yourself in perfect health, your subconscious mind will start to believe that it is true, and you will attract that reality into your life. To begin, take a few deep breaths and close your eyes. Imagine yourself full of energy, vibrant, and happy. See yourself engaging in your favorite activities and feeling amazing. Hold this image in your mind for a few minutes and repeat this practice regularly.

One way to enhance your visualization practice is to use guided meditations specifically designed for health visualization. You can find these online or in guided meditation apps. For example, a guided meditation for visualizing perfect health might ask you to visualize a bright light entering your body and filling you with healing energy. As you visualize this light, you might also repeat positive affirmations to yourself, such as "I am healthy and strong."

In addition to visualization, it's important to take action towards your health goals. The Law of Attraction can help to create miracles, but it's also important to support your body with healthy habits and practices. This might include eating a nutritious diet, getting regular exercise, and engaging in self-care practices that support your physical, emotional, and spiritual well-being. By combining visualization with healthy habits, you can create a powerful synergy that helps you to achieve optimal health and well-being.

Positive Affirmations for Health:

Affirmations have been used for centuries to reprogram the subconscious mind and align our thoughts and emotions with our desires. The power of affirmations lies in their ability to shape our beliefs, attitudes, and behaviors by creating new neural pathways in our brains. When we repeat positive affirmations related to health and well-being, we send a message to our subconscious mind that we are capable of achieving optimal health and vitality.

One of the most important aspects of affirmations is the language we use. It's essential to frame our affirmations in a positive light and avoid negative language such as "I am not sick" or "I am not in pain." Instead, we should focus on what we want to achieve, such as "I am healthy and vibrant" or "I am pain-free and full of energy." This positive framing helps us to create a more positive outlook and attract more positivity into our lives.

Another key element of affirmations is repetition. It's important to repeat our affirmations regularly, either silently or out loud, to reinforce the positive message we are sending to our subconscious mind. By repeating our affirmations consistently, we can begin to shift our mindset and beliefs about our health and well-being.

Finally, it's important to practice affirmations with intention and mindfulness. We should choose affirmations that resonate with us personally and align with our goals and desires. It's also helpful to set aside time each day to focus on our affirmations and visualize ourselves achieving our desired outcomes. By doing so, we can tap into the power of our subconscious mind and manifest the health and vitality we desire.

Here are some additional examples of health-related affirmations that you can use to enhance your well-being:

My body is strong, healthy, and resilient.

I am full of vibrant energy and vitality.

I radiate good health and well-being.

I am grateful for my body and all that it does for me.

I trust my body's ability to heal itself.

Every cell in my body is vibrating with health and vitality.

I am at peace with my body and mind.

I am free from pain and discomfort.

I am filled with love and compassion for myself and others.

I am living a life full of health, happiness, and abundance.

Affirmations are a powerful tool for improving our health and well-being. By using positive language, repeating our affirmations regularly, and practicing them with intention and mindfulness, we can reprogram our subconscious mind and attract more health and vitality into our lives.

Gratitude for Health: Gratitude is an incredibly powerful emotion that has been shown to have numerous health benefits. It can shift our energy field from negative to positive, attracting more positivity and abundance into our lives. By focusing on the things we are grateful for, we can improve our overall well-being and promote healing in our bodies.

There are many ways to practice gratitude. One simple way is to take a few moments each day to write down or think about the things you are grateful for in your life. This could be anything from your health and family to the roof over your head and the food on your table. Here are some other examples of how you can exercise gratitude in your daily life:

Gratitude journal: Start a gratitude journal where you write down the things you are grateful for each day. This is a great way to reflect on the positive aspects of your life and focus on the good things.

Gratitude meditation: Set aside some time each day to meditate on the things you are grateful for. Focus on your breath and allow yourself to feel gratitude for the blessings in your life.

Gratitude jar: Create a gratitude jar where you write down something you are grateful for each day on a slip of paper and put it in the jar. Over time, you can look back at all the things you have written down and reflect on the positive aspects of your life.

Gratitude letter: Write a letter to someone you are grateful for, expressing your gratitude for their presence in your life. This can be a powerful exercise in cultivating gratitude and strengthening your relationships.

By incorporating gratitude into your daily life, you can shift your energy towards positivity and abundance, promoting healing and well-being in your body and mind.

The Law of Attraction and the power of positive thinking can have a profound impact on our overall health and well-being. These concepts can be applied to every aspect of our lives, including our physical, mental, and emotional health. By harnessing the power of our thoughts and beliefs, we can create miracles and even cure diseases that were once deemed incurable.

It's important to note that the Law of Attraction is not a replacement for medical treatment or professional advice. It is meant to be used in conjunction with these things, as a complementary approach to healing. With that said, let's dive into how the Law of Attraction can positively impact our health.

Our thoughts and beliefs are incredibly powerful. They have the ability to shape our reality and influence the outcomes we experience in our lives. When it comes to our health, our thoughts and beliefs can impact our physical, mental, and emotional well-being. If we constantly think and worry about getting sick, we may actually attract illness into our lives. Our negative thoughts and fears can weaken our immune system and make us more susceptible to getting sick. On the other hand, if we focus on health and wellness, we can attract positive outcomes and create a stronger, healthier body and mind.

The Law of Attraction works on the principle that we can manifest our desires and goals by focusing our thoughts and energy on them. By using this same principle, we can also manifest good health and a disease-free body. This may seem like a far-fetched idea, but numerous studies have shown that our thoughts and beliefs can have a direct impact on our physical health.

One of the first steps to harnessing the power of the Law of Attraction for our health is to let go of negative thoughts. Negative thoughts and emotions can have a profound impact on our physical health. By letting go of negative thoughts and emotions, we free up space for positive energy and health to flow into our lives. We can practice mindfulness and meditation to become more aware of our thoughts and emotions. When negative thoughts or emotions arise, we can acknowledge them and let them go. Focusing on positive thoughts and emotions can help us attract more health and well-being into our lives.

Another important step in harnessing the power of the Law of Attraction for our health is to practice self-care. Taking care of our physical and emotional well-being is crucial for good health. By practicing self-care activities like meditation, yoga, or regular exercise, we can reduce stress, promote relaxation, and boost our energy levels. These activities can also help us develop a sense of inner peace and contentment, which can have a positive impact on our overall well-being.

Trusting the universe is also a crucial aspect of the Law of Attraction. By trusting that the universe has our best interests at heart, we can let go of fear and anxiety and attract more positive energy into our lives. Trusting the universe means believing that we are worthy of good health and well-being. We can let go of negative thoughts and trust that the universe has our back. By doing so, we can attract good health and well-being into our lives.

Conclusion: Taking care of our physical health is crucial in addition to utilizing the techniques of the Law of Attraction. This involves maintaining a healthy diet, exercising regularly, and getting enough rest and sleep. By doing so, we establish a strong foundation for the Law of Attraction to work effectively.

In conclusion, the Law of Attraction is a powerful tool for improving our health and well-being. By being mindful of our thoughts and beliefs, practicing affirmations, visualization, and gratitude, as well as taking care of our physical health, we can achieve positive outcomes, and even heal ourselves from diseases that were once considered incurable. The key is to believe in the power of the Law of Attraction and have faith in the process of healing.

In summary, by applying the Law of Attraction, we can attract optimal health and well-being into our lives. By focusing on positive thoughts and emotions, letting go of negativity, and having trust in the universe, we can create a happier and healthier life. It's important to keep in mind that the connection between the mind and body is a powerful tool, and our thoughts and emotions can significantly impact our physical health.

However, it's essential to note that the Law of Attraction is not a substitute for medical treatment or advice. If experiencing health problems, seeking advice from a qualified medical professional is always important. Nevertheless, by combining the Law of Attraction with medical treatment, we can enhance our healing process.

Ultimately, the Law of Attraction can be a potent tool for achieving optimal health and well-being. By aligning our thoughts, emotions, and energy with our desires, we can manifest good health and even cure diseases that were previously thought to be incurable. Practicing self-care, releasing negative thoughts, and having faith in the universe are essential in attracting good health and well-being into our lives.

Chapter 19. Conclusion: The Power of the Law of Attraction to Think Like and Become a Millionaire

In this book, we have explored the power of the law of attraction and how you can use it to think like a millionaire and become one. We have covered key concepts such as the millionaire mindset, visualization, vision boards, affirmations, goal setting and action planning, and overcoming limiting beliefs and obstacles.

By following the strategies outlined in this book, you can train your brain to think like a millionaire and attract wealth and success into your life. It is important to remember that the law of attraction is a powerful tool, but it is only one part of the equation. You must also take action and be committed to your goals in order to achieve financial success.

The journey to becoming a millionaire may not be easy, but it is possible. With hard work, persistence, and a positive attitude, you can overcome obstacles and achieve your financial goals. So start today by setting specific, measurable goals, creating a vision board, and using affirmations to train your brain to think like a millionaire.

Remember, wealth and success are within reach. By embracing the law of attraction and taking action, you can become a millionaire and live the life of your dreams.

Chapter 19. Summary of Key Takeaways

In this chapter, we will summarize the key takeaways from the previous chapters in "Think like a Millionaire." The goal of this chapter is to provide a quick reference for readers who want to quickly review the main concepts covered in the book.

1. Overview of the Law of Attraction

The law of attraction states that we attract into our lives what we focus on and believe.

By focusing on positive thoughts and beliefs, we can attract abundance and prosperity into our lives.

2. The Millionaire Mindset

The millionaire mindset is characterized by a positive and abundant mindset, a strong sense of purpose, and a commitment to continuous learning and personal growth.

To develop the millionaire mindset, you must adopt a positive and abundant outlook, focus on your strengths, and cultivate a strong sense of purpose.

3. A. The Science of Attraction

The science of attraction is based on the concept of the law of attraction and the power of the mind to influence our thoughts and beliefs.

By understanding the science of attraction, you can learn to harness the power of your mind to attract abundance and prosperity into your life.

4. How to Train Your Brain to Think Like a Millionaire

To train your brain to think like a millionaire, you must focus on positive thoughts and beliefs, cultivate a strong sense of purpose, and adopt a growth mindset.

By using visualization, vision boards, affirmations, and positive self-talk, you can train your brain to think like a millionaire and attract abundance into your life.

5. The Importance of Visualizing Your Goals

Visualizing your goals is a powerful way to attract abundance and prosperity into your life.

By visualizing your goals, you can train your brain to focus on your desired outcome and increase your motivation to take action.

6. Creating a Vision Board

A vision board is a visual representation of your goals and aspirations.

By creating a vision board, you can keep your goals and aspirations at the forefront of your mind and attract abundance into your life.

7. Visualizing in a Half-Trance State

Visualizing in a half-trance state can help you tap into the subconscious mind and attract abundance into your life.

To visualize in a half-trance state, you must focus on your breath, relax your body, and visualize your goals and aspirations in detail.

8. Affirmations and Positive Self-Talk

Affirmations and positive self-talk are powerful tools for attracting abundance and prosperity into your life.

By using affirmations and positive self-talk, you can cultivate a positive and abundant mindset and train your brain to think like a millionaire.

9. Crafting Powerful Affirmations for Wealth and Success

To craft powerful affirmations for wealth and success, you must focus on positive and empowering statements that align with your goals and aspirations.

By crafting powerful affirmations, you can attract abundance and prosperity into your life.

10. Implementing Affirmations into Your Daily Routine

To implement affirmations into your daily routine, you must make them a regular part of your day, such as first thing in the morning or before bed.

By implementing affirmations into your daily routine, you can train your brain to think positively and attract abundance into your life.

11. Goal Setting and Action Planning

Goal setting and action planning are essential for attracting abundance and prosperity into your life.

By setting specific, measurable goals and taking action to achieve them, you can attract abundance and prosperity into your life.

Chapter 20: Conclusion - The Path to Millionaire Thinking and Living

In this book, we have explored the Law of Attraction and its powerful impact on wealth and success. By understanding the science of attraction and developing a millionaire mindset, you can harness the power of your thoughts and beliefs to attract abundance into your life.

We have examined the importance of visualization and goal setting, the benefits of affirmations and positive self-talk, and strategies for overcoming limiting beliefs and obstacles.

In order to make the most of the Law of Attraction, it is important to have a clear understanding of what you want and to take consistent, focused action towards your goals. Remember that wealth and success are not just about money – they also encompass health, relationships, and happiness.

As you embark on this journey of millionaire thinking and living, it is important to be patient and persistent. Success is not a destination, but a journey. Embrace the process and be open to new opportunities and experiences.

Remember that you are the master of your own thoughts and beliefs, and that you have the power to shape your reality. By continuing to focus on your goals, visualize success, and take action towards your dreams, you will be able to achieve the life of your dreams.

The key takeaways from this book are:

The Law of Attraction is a powerful force that can help you attract wealth and success into your life

Developing a millionaire mindset and positive beliefs is crucial for success

Visualization, affirmations, and goal setting are powerful tools for attracting abundance

Overcoming limiting beliefs and obstacles is an important part of the journey

Consistent, focused action is necessary to bring your goals to life.

We hope that this book has provided you with valuable insights and practical strategies for thinking like a millionaire and living a life of abundance. The path to success and wealth is open to you – all you have to do is take the first step.

The "Bonus Section" of the book is an additional section that provides readers with additional resources and information to support their journey towards millionaire thinking and living. This section may include things like:

Worksheets and exercises to help readers put what they have learned into practice

Additional tips and strategies for using the Law of Attraction to attract wealth and success

149

Inspiring success stories from individuals who have used the Law of Attraction to transform their lives

Recommendations for further reading and resources for personal growth and development.

This bonus section serves as a supplement to the main content of the book, providing readers with additional tools and information to support their journey towards millionaire thinking and living.

Chapter 21: Meditation for Wealth and Abundance

Introduction:

Meditation has long been recognized as a powerful tool for promoting physical, mental, and emotional well-being. In this chapter, we will explore the role that meditation can play in attracting wealth and abundance into your life. By incorporating regular meditation practices into your daily routine, you can tap into the power of the Law of Attraction and manifest the financial success and abundance that you desire.

The Benefits of Meditation for Wealth and Abundance:

There are many ways in which meditation can support your journey towards wealth and abundance. Some of the key benefits include:

Increased clarity and focus: By taking time to quiet your mind and focus on your breathing, you can develop greater clarity and focus. This can help you to stay motivated and on track towards your financial goals, even in the face of obstacles and setbacks.

Increased positive thinking and self-esteem: Meditation can help you to cultivate a positive mindset, reduce stress, and increase feelings of self-worth and self-esteem. By feeling

151

good about yourself, you will be better equipped to attract the abundance and success you desire.

Improved visualization skills: Meditation can help you to develop and improve your visualization skills. By regularly visualizing your desired outcomes, you can bring your goals and desires closer to your reality.

How to Practice Meditation for Wealth and Abundance:

To get the most out of meditation for wealth and abundance, it is important to practice regularly. Here are some steps you can follow to get started:

Choose a quiet, peaceful place where you won't be disturbed.

Sit comfortably and close your eyes.

Focus on your breathing and allow your mind to become still.

Visualize yourself surrounded by abundance and prosperity. See yourself in a happy, secure financial situation, with enough money to do all the things you want to do.

Repeat positive affirmations to yourself, such as "I am rich and successful," "Money flows easily into my life," or "I deserve abundance and prosperity."

Continue meditating for as long as feels comfortable, usually between 10 to 20 minutes.

Conclusion:

Meditation is a powerful tool for attracting wealth and abundance into your life. By incorporating regular meditation practices into your daily routine, you can tap into the power of the Law of Attraction, increase your positive thinking, and improve your visualization skills. Whether you are just starting out on your journey towards wealth and abundance or are looking to deepen your existing practices, meditation can help you to manifest the financial success and prosperity that you desire.

Chapter 22 "The Law of Attraction and Money Mindset Masterclass"

Introduction:

The Law of Attraction and Money Mindset Masterclass is a comprehensive program designed to help you understand and apply the principles of the Law of Attraction in your life, specifically in the area of wealth and abundance. The program is designed to take you on a journey of self-discovery, where you will learn how to train your brain to think like a millionaire and attract more money into your life.

Module 1: Understanding the Law of Attraction

In this module, you will dive deeper into the science of the Law of Attraction and how it works. You will learn about the different laws of the universe, such as the Law of Vibration, the Law of Attraction, and the Law of Allowance, and how they relate to your financial well-being. You will also learn how your thoughts and emotions affect your reality and how you can use the Law of Attraction to create the life you desire.

Module 2: The Millionaire Mindset

This module will focus on developing a millionaire mindset. You will learn about the beliefs and habits that successful and wealthy people possess, and how you can adopt these traits to attract more money into your life. You will also learn about the power of visualization and affirmations and how they can help you manifest your desired financial outcomes.

Module 3: The Science of Attraction

In this module, you will delve into the science of attraction and learn about the role that your thoughts, emotions, and beliefs play in creating your reality. You will learn about the power of positive thinking and how it can help you attract more money into your life. You will also learn about the importance of mindfulness and meditation, and how they can help you stay focused on your goals.

Module 4: Creating a Vision Board

In this module, you will learn about the power of visualization and how you can use it to attract more money into your life. You will learn how to create a vision board and use it to manifest your desired financial outcomes. You will also learn about the importance of having specific, measurable goals and how to use your vision board to help you achieve them.

Module 5: Affirmations and Positive Self-Talk

In this module, you will learn about the power of affirmations and positive self-talk and how you can use them to attract more money into your life. You will learn how to craft powerful affirmations that align with your goals and how to use them in your daily routine to manifest your desired financial outcomes.

Module 6: Implementing Affirmations into Your Daily Routine

In this module, you will learn about the importance of implementing affirmations into your daily routine. You will learn how to make affirmations a part of your daily life, and how to use them to reprogram your subconscious mind and attract more money into your life.

Module 7: Goal Setting and Action Planning

In this module, you will learn about the importance of goal setting and action planning. You will learn how to set specific, measurable, achievable, relevant, and time-bound (SMART) goals, and how to create an action plan to achieve them. You will also learn about the importance of taking action and how to stay motivated and focused on your goals.

Module 8: Overcoming Limiting Beliefs and Obstacles

In this module, you will learn about the limiting beliefs that hold you back from attracting more money into your life. You will learn how to identify and overcome these limiting beliefs and how to deal with obstacles and setbacks that may arise on your path to financial freedom.

Chapter 23: The Law of Attraction and Money Mindset Advanced Masterclass

In this chapter, we will delve deeper into the specific steps you can take to fully embody the millionaire mindset and attract abundance and prosperity into your life. This section will serve as a comprehensive masterclass, covering all the key elements of the Law of Attraction and how to apply them to your financial situation.

First, we will review the basics of the Law of Attraction, including the importance of focusing your thoughts and emotions on what you want to attract, rather than what you don't want. We will also touch upon the power of gratitude, and how focusing on what you are grateful for can help you manifest more of what you want.

Next, we will explore the specific money-related mindset shifts you need to make in order to start attracting wealth and abundance. This will include understanding your relationship with money, shifting your beliefs about abundance, and developing a prosperity consciousness.

We will also cover the importance of taking inspired action, and how to align your thoughts, emotions, and actions with your goals. This includes setting specific, measurable, and achievable goals, and taking action towards them on a daily basis.

Finally, we will discuss the role of visualization and affirmations in manifesting wealth and abundance. We will go through various visualization and affirmation techniques, and show you how to integrate them into your daily routine for maximum effectiveness.

By the end of this section, you will have a clear understanding of how to harness the power of the Law of Attraction to attract abundance and prosperity into your life, and have all the tools you need to start thinking and acting like a millionaire.

Chapter 24: Tools and Resources for Continued Growth and Success

The journey towards becoming a millionaire through the law of attraction is not a one-time event, but a continuous process of growth and development. In order to maintain and enhance the mindset and habits that will lead to success, it is important to have access to resources and tools that will support your ongoing efforts.

A. Books and Audio Resources: There are many books and audio resources available on the law of attraction, personal growth, and wealth creation. These resources can provide you with new insights and ideas to help you stay motivated and on track towards your goals.

B. Online Courses and Workshops: Online courses and workshops can provide you with in-depth training and instruction on specific aspects of the law of attraction, such as goal setting, visualization, and affirmations. These courses can be a great way to deepen your understanding of these concepts and gain new skills and techniques to help you manifest your goals.

C. Support Communities: Joining a support community can provide you with the opportunity to connect with like-minded individuals who are also on the path towards financial freedom. These communities can provide you with encouragement, support, and accountability, which can be especially helpful when you encounter challenges and setbacks along the way.

D. Coaching and Mentorship: Working with a coach or mentor can provide you with personalized guidance and support as you work to achieve your financial goals. This type of one-on-one support can help you stay motivated, overcome obstacles, and make faster progress towards your goals.

E. Personal Development Tools: Personal development tools such as journals, planners, and vision boards can be extremely helpful in keeping you focused and on track towards your goals. Regularly reviewing your goals and progress can help you stay motivated and on track towards your desired outcomes.

In conclusion, having access to a variety of tools and resources can help you maintain and enhance the millionaire mindset and habits that will lead to your success. As you continue on your journey towards financial freedom, take advantage of these resources and tools to stay focused, motivated, and on track towards your goals.

Back Cover:

This book is a must-read for anyone seeking inspiration and guidance on how to overcome obstacles and achieve success. Join Tony Tushar Popat on his journey towards finding success and happiness, and learn the principles and techniques that have helped him achieve his goals. Whether you are a student, a professional, or an entrepreneur, this book is for you. Don't miss out on this opportunity to transform your life and achieve your dreams.